with love &
Thanks
Catherine X

LET'S GET IT ON

The Politics of Black Performance

Edited by Catherine Ugwu

Institute of Contemporary Arts, London
Bay Press, Seattle

Let's Get it On
The Politics of Black Performance

Bay Press, Seattle
ICA, London

This publication was funded with assistance from the Gulbenkian
Foundation and the Arts Council of England

The Institute of Contemporary Arts is sponsored by Toshiba and financially assisted by
the Arts Council of England, Westminster City Council and the British Film Institute.
Educational charity registered number 236848

ISBN Bay Press 0-941920-33-X
(USA & World rights excluding UK & Ireland)
Bay Press
115 West Denny Way
Seattle
WA 98119-4205
USA
Tel 206 284 5913
Fax 206 284 1218

ISBN ICA 0-905263-64-2
(UK & Ireland)
ICA Publications
12 Carlton House Terrace
London SW1Y 5AH
UK
Tel 171 930 0493
Fax 171 873 0051

British Library cataloguing-in-publication data.
A catalogue record for this book is available from the British Library

Library of Congress No. 95-15190

This book has been published with the generous financial assistance of

The Calouste Gulbenkian Foundation

The Arts Council of England

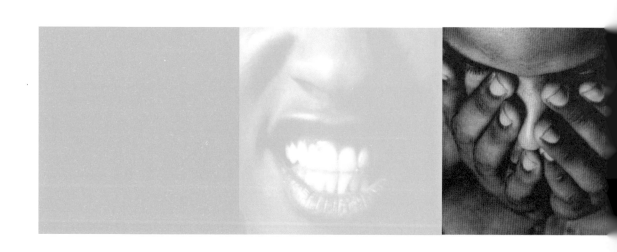

CONTENTS

Dedicated to my niece Olima Lauren Ugwu-Rolfe born 7th July 1993.

With thanks to all the artists whose work, past and present, inspired this publication and all the artists and writers whose contributions make up this book, as well as those who have kindly lent photographs and provided information about their work over the last six months.

I am eternally grateful to the Calouste Gulbenkian Foundation, the Combined Arts Department of The Arts Council of England and Bay Press, whose support and financial assistance helped realise this publication.

Thanks to all at the ICA, Garfield Allen, Alex Ankrah, David A Bailey, Paula Brown, Fiona Ellis, Georgina Evans, Rachel Gibson, Eleanor Grant, Stella Hall, Bush Hartshorn, Martin Hudson, Barbara Hunt, Isaac Julien, John Keiffer, Kobena Mercer, Nikki Milican, Jordan Peimer, Tony Rolfe, Joanna Scanlan, Jill Scott, Sonia Serafin, Sally Stote, SuAndi, Diane Warden, Bob Wisdom and Rosalind Ugwu, all of whose actions have in one way or another contributed to the realisation of this collection.

Thanks to Keith Khan who, along with Lois Keidan, convinced me to take on this important project and helped formulate the initial ideas; Ali Zaidi, photographer for the ICA's 1993 Respect season; Robert Taylor for his remarkably sensitive photographs for this publication and Yumi Matote for her design. Thanks to Katy Sender, Melissa Larner, Helena Reckitt and Alan Read for their invaluable advice, comments and intellectual support. Thanks also to all the artists whose work has challenged and inspired audiences at the ICA over the last two years and to the ICA Live Arts team, Pat Elliott, Rachel Shipp and Justin O'Shaughnessy whose skills, commitment and enthusiasm have helped so many artists in the presentation and development of their work.

Thanks to Kim Lau, Lenore Craggs, Rossen Daskalov, Wiz, Susan Lewis, Kim Sweet, Tamzin Griffin, Victor Freeman, Anthony Green and my mother, Brenda Ugwu for their belief and friendship.

Special thanks to Andrea Phillips, Sub-editor and Production Manager, and Ragnar Farr, ICA Publications Co-ordinator, whose dedication, skill and unfailing optimism saw this publication to completion. Finally Lois Keidan without whose wisdom, guidance and friendship this publication would not exist.

INTRODUCTION
Catherine Ugwu

Let's Get it On is a provocative examination of issues of cultural identity through an investigation of innovative performance practice. It charts the emergence and evolution over the last decade of politicised black British and American live art, documenting and discussing existing work in relation to wider political concerns. Recent years have witnessed the emergence of a new generation of artists who are negotiating difference and new contexts for creativity. *Let's Get it On* attempts to highlight the ways that, at this particular historical moment, performance practitioners are commenting on and influencing the wider political and social realities of our time. It aims to explore the complexities of identity formulation and difference by locating them in the work of individual artists. The main papers therefore attempt to provide a political and cultural context for this work. The artists' pages, which make up a substantial and important part of this document, reflect the diversity of voices operating within current practice[1].

Let's Get it On, produced by ICA Live Arts, one of five programming departments at the Institute of Contemporary Arts, London, has evolved from debates and practices which have been central to ICA Live Arts current artistic policy. Witnessing the appearance of a broad range of artists who are boldly fronting issues of identity and notions of difference in their work, ICA Live Arts has reflected this development by supporting and nurturing these artists and their work.

Over the last ten years, live art in Britain and the USA has been in pursuit of new ways of representing and responding to our shifting times. A range of practices - from theatre to installation, film to music, visual art to dance - have crossed each others' paths and

blurred each others' edges. In the process, these practices have opened up the possibility of discussing new agendas through mixing artforms, unrestrained by tradition or convention.

Live art in Britain - perhaps better described by the more generalised term 'performance' in the USA - exists at the centre of this process. Not an artistic discipline in the formal sense, live art embraces a broad cultural church which often defies definition. It is this very resistance to categorisation and containment, along with its ability to surprise and unnerve, which makes live art's impact so far-reaching.

Within this fluidity there are, however, some markers that can be traced across a range of work that has emerged over the last few decades. Conceptual in nature, the work is invariably driven by the expression of ideas rather than the desire to display particular skills. It usually draws on the artists themselves as source material rather than creating fictional others. It incorporates and fuses a range of media. It is incessantly concerned with images of the moment; any cultural symbol, reference or icon is appropriated and subverted; the world is up for grabs. Process, context and site are significant, as is the direct and unmediated interaction between the artist and the viewer. The raw and naked exposure of the artist is bound up with the live presence of the viewer. The experience is invariably ephemeral, the only evidence following the event existing in the memories and imaginations of both artist and audience.

Over the years, performance artists have taken on many aspects of the human condition, often at the greatest risk to themselves. Yet this area of practice seems to remain a footnote to British and American cultural life. Under-funded, under-sung, unrecognised, its presence is becoming more pertinent as the questions it poses become more urgent. As we move towards the close of one century and the beginning of another, artists continue to find avenues for expression unencumbered by restrictions of form, practice, belief or tradition. It is this very freedom to be or act by any means necessary which makes live art impossible to contain, ignore or restrain. This makes the question 'what is live art?' even harder to answer. As I'm sure the artists and contributors to this publication and this area of practice would respond, it is not so much *what* it is but what it can *do* that is important.

In the context of a wide range of identity-related critical writing, particularly in the area of black cultural practice, the impact of black live art and related practices has continually been negated.

It is work without an historical context or critical framework, and is often perceived as operating at the margins of society. It is for these reasons, amongst others, that ICA Live Arts felt this publication was long overdue and could contribute to the process of a whole body of work by a people compelled to write themselves into being. This is an attempt to make the invisible visible.

The issues of colonialism and de-colonisation with which this publication engages are universal and have global significance. It would be an impossible and monumental task to attempt to deal with contemporary cultural practice around the world. *Let's Get it On,* therefore, focuses on performance practice which has emerged from the dense multicultural centres.of Britain and the USA. The historical legacies and acts of cultural resistance articulated in this publication reflect the complexity of black cultural experience and hint at what forms and shapes it. It is hoped that, although only dealing with two nations, the publication highlights the importance of transcending nationality to develop an understanding of the elaborate and complicated factors which influence identity formation.

We hope this publication will be of interest and use to those actively engaged in cultural practice. By necessity its frame of cultural reference is broad and should therefore appeal to artists, audiences and students as well as critics, academics, producers and funders.

Catherine Ugwu
Editor

1   One contentious issue raised many times within this publication is the use of the word black and indeed its spelling. Many terms or expressions could have been used throughout this publication. The general editorial position has been to use the term black (with a lower case *b*) as referring to peoples of African, Asian, South East Asian, Latino (Puerto Rican, Mexican, Cuban) or Native American descent.

12

'... to be real'   Paul Gilroy
The dissident forms
of black expressive
culture

'...TO BE REAL'
The dissident forms of black expressive culture

Paul Gilroy

The circle of the dance is a permissive circle: it protects and permits. At certain times on certain days, men and women come together at a given place, and there, under the solemn eyes of the tribe, fling themselves into a seemingly unorganized pantomime, which is in reality extremely systematic, in which by various means - shakes of the head, bending of the spinal column, throwing the whole body backwards - may be deciphered as in an open book the huge effort of a community to exorcise itself, to liberate itself, to explain itself. There are no limits - inside the circle. Frantz Fanon

And so we enact for ourselves theatrical scenes, on the stage of our continued wandering, such that it can appear ridiculous to recommend to us the value of self-analysis provided by theatrical activity. Edouard Glissant

The interface between black cultural practice and black political aspirations has been a curious and wonderfully durable modern phenomenon. This dynamic link, which has supplied so much of the moral resonance to contemporary dissident movements, formed far from its own abject source, dissolves the discrete fixity of culture and politics. It was first established long ago, appearing in catastrophic conditions, where the creative recycling and adaptation of pre-colonial, African forms simultaneously offered both accommodation to, and transcendence of slavery and the plantation governmentality that had been based on rationally applied terrors as much as pragmatic banditry. The connection between expressive culture and liberatory politics was nurtured. It has been joyously rediscovered and reinvented repeatedly since, as part of a complex and ambivalent response to the successive waves of absolutely traumatic modernisation that followed slavery and ran onwards from the brutal origins of capitalism, through its

colonial phases, to its contemporary overdevelopment. Sometimes compressed, sometimes attenuated, that vital connection was maintained even when the institution of modern racial slavery gave way to the industrialisation it had fostered. It persisted though slavery was abolished and economic, social and cultural life were recomposed on the dubious bases provided by those modern, formal freedoms that could exist without democracy.

In these embattled circumstances expressive arts acquired a threefold character. They reconciled their producers to their sublime plight and offered them a measure of compensation for it while also providing a partial refuge from its most malevolent effects. Their art combined the laments of unfreedom with its oppressed confirmation. This distinctive aporetic blend founded a tradition of culture-making that resists the verdict of redundancy to which its own bleak history points. That observation is as near as the study of modern black expressive cultures gets to producing a meta-theory of its own functioning. In this post-colonial mood, there should be no sentimental celebration of pure alterity mechanistically producing pure culture as pure resistance.

The living, non-traditional tradition of black vernacular self-fashioning, culture-making, play and antiphonic communal conversation is complex and complicated by its historic relationship to the covert public worlds of a subaltern modernity. The slaves, like many other conquered and colonised peoples, were gradually and not always reluctantly, drawn into the world that their owners defined and regulated by more than merely coercive means. As they internalised the new languages, causal and purposive understandings, spiritual codes, spatial and temporal perceptions upon which their survival was

'... to be real' Paul Gilroy
The dissident forms
of black expressive
culture

conditional, as well as the orientation towards nature and the natural world that their masters and mistresses required, they did not necessarily abandon the alternative non-European habits that were condensed into living memories of an anterior history and social life. Indeed, these residual habits were often reproduced in customary form even when their earlier 'traditional' meanings had been forgotten, were changed or no longer immediately relevant[1]. Nowhere were the masters, mistresses and other beneficiaries of slavery and colonialism successful in insulating their own lifeworlds absolutely from the disruptive and contaminating effects produced by those they dominated, but upon whom, perversely, they were dependent. The dominant groups were always themselves transformed by the historically novel conditions of their dominance. In particular, they were affected by an uneasy intimacy in which their slaves, bondspeople and servants - stubbornly neither strangers, nor friends - were able to shift the fulcrum around which the interests of these by-now-racialised groups moved, seeking equilibrium but never finding it for long enough to claim reliable stability.

The relatively simple understanding of cultural differences that supplied the Manichean cornerstones of the colonial world gave way gradually to an infinitely shaded, protean and unquiet system of differentiation and unequal cultural exchanges that might warrant the term post-colonial. Recognising this change should not erase or even unduly qualify the wrongs, injustices and foundational brutality of these bitter, and still poorly understood historical processes. The complexity of these social and cultural relationships should provide neither an alibi for quiescence nor an excuse for indifference. Comprehending contemporary developments in and around performance culture requires that we do not yield to the impulse to deny, and thereby over-simplify, the volatile dynamics of the ongoing processes that are half-grasped by incomplete concepts like creolisation, syncretism and 'hybridity'.

Survival in slave regimes or in other extreme conditions intrinsic to colonial order promoted the acquisition of what we might now understand to be performance skills, and refined the appreciation of mimesis by both dominant and dominated. Apart from the work involved in enacting their servitude and inferiority while guarding their autonomy, people found significant everyday triumphs by mimicking and in a sense mastering, their rulers and conquerors, masters and mistresses. Some even escaped slavery by passing for white. The exploits of Frederick Douglass and William and Ellen Craft are only the most celebrated tales of slaves who fled bondage in disguise. The account of Ellen's thespian skills in crossing the lines of both 'race' and gender provide an especially memorable and pertinent example, having been written and published in London[2]. This characteristic drama was developed close to the powerful bodies that were simultaneously serviced and manipulated. It was elaborated in the covert social arena that became the public world of oppositional identity. The dramaturgy of power that haunts today's racial politics and contemporary expressive cultural codes was first 'formatted' in those grim locations. It has subsequently been endowed with a variety of incompatible contents - all of them enabled by the bloody 'intialization' of that subaltern modernity.

There are many histories still to be told and written about the undervalued and underanalysed experiences of cultural and aesthetic fusion and mutation that began the transformation of that discrepant modernity into marginal modernisms. They have often been wrongly excluded from critical discussions about modernity, its uneven consolidation or possible eclipse, let alone its aesthetic character and creative opportunities. Performance was central to the process of cultural intermixture.

I am introducing a collection of writings on contemporary black live art performance with a reminder of the significance of inter-, trans- and cross-cultural history, not because some unbroken continuity or essential connectedness between today's mongrel dynamics and past purities is being suggested here as a special interpretive device or ethical yardstick. No straight or unbroken line of descent through either gendered line can establish plausible genealogical relations between current forms and moods and their fixed, identifiable and authentic origins. It is rather that the forbidding density of the processes of conquest, accommodation, mediation and interpenetration that helps to define colonial cultures also demands that we re-conceptualise the whole problematic of origins. This should be done in ways that reject the unhelpful but sadly fashionable suggestion that cultural forms and habits have an ordered and predictable evolution from pure to impure, from simple to complex. Our difficult object: black performance culture and its social and political forms is a profane practice. It has been propagated by

'... to be real'
The dissident forms
of black expressive
culture

Paul Gilroy

unpredictable means in non-linear patterns. Promiscuity is the key principle of its continuance.

The pattern of communication found in the unstable colonial world was governed by radical contingency. The civility of the slaves, the colonised and their descendants remains sly. Their signifyin(g) and shape-shifting can still be tactical as well as playful; contestatory as well as compensatory. Creolised creativity entered the arterial system of the modern body politic via the capillaries of popular culture. It made resistance and accommodation into inseparable twins: different possibilities that correspond precisely, but not in a simple mechanism which specifies that more of one means less of the other. Minstrelsy provided the site of this fateful confluence. Recognising this double quality ought to be central to all accounts of the performance traditions of new world blacks and their relation to the history of the cultural industries. It should also be indispensable to contemporary assessments of the cultural politics of 'race'. It is being addressed as an important theme in the revisionist histories of minstrelsy in the United States that will hopefully be followed by equivalent studies in this country[3]. To read this complexity as the simple power of a latent but omnipotent Africanity, manipulating the superficial communicative codes that are manifest within white supremacy, is to trivialise the urgent question of cross-cultural trafficking and to obscure its potential and actual political effects. This could be disastrous now that white youth are affiliated in their millions to the outer-national intra-cultural phenomenon that is the hip hop nation[4] though that affiliation does not necessarily induce them to transcend racialised ontology or perception.

Paul Lawrence Dunbar, the African-American poet who was also the first black person to support himself financially as a professional writer, captured something of the elemental force of this constitutive ambivalence in his celebrated poem *We wear the mask*. He comments acutely upon the institution of minstrelsy, while also managing to convey both the stresses and the opportunities that can arise from refining the ability to manipulate the expectations of whites who are conditioned and misled by the consistency with which those whom they dominate (and on whom they depend) deploy the mask effect:

Pages 18&19
**The Black and White
Minstrel Show**
Photo courtesy of
BBC Picture Archives

We wear the mask that grins and lies,
It hides our cheeks and shades our eyes,
This debt we pay to human guile;
With torn and bleeding hearts we smile,
And mouth with myriad subtleties.
Why should the world be otherwise,
In counting all our tears and sighs?
Nay, let them only see us, while
We wear the mask.[5]

It would appear that any subversive or 'disruptive' communicative opportunities can co-exist with the painful demands made upon black subjects by the everyday politics of white supremacy. Those small everyday triumphs and a welcome measure of social integrity numb the chronic pain experienced as a result of internal exile from modernity. This is of special significance to contemporary black artists who operate within a more extensive cultural circuitry than the one that Dunbar knew. It is worth emphasising that white supremacy and other forms of racialised knowledge touched but were not able to determine the character of the black cultural and artistic productions that were often directed against their brittle authority. The discursive formations of racialised authority have changed their forms over time: evolving and re-combining their deterministic logics in order to rationalise, legitimise and explain. The political languages of 'race', biology and culture may become congruent but they have also been known to conflict. The sheer existence of black creativity sets a problem for them to explain. Black art, vernacular and otherwise, has answered all of them. However, the outlaw creativity of the would-be mask manipulators exceeds the mocking replies which their works offer to white power and white knowledge. The feral spirit of this art disseminates a special kind of dissidence in which performance and what Judith Butler, following her Nietzschean path through speech act theory, calls performativity: 'the discursive mode by which ontological effects are installed'[6], are important and embattled.

It is here that the question of identity emerges as fundamental. Without going deeply into

'… to be real'   Paol Gilroy
The dissident forms
of black expressive
culture

Fun Da Mental in concert
Photo: Matt Bright,
courtesy of
Nation Records Ltd

the life and death stakes raised by this over-charged term and the diverse political interests - national and supra-national, sub-national, transnational and anti-national - from which it is currently inextricable, it seems appropriate to point out that the concept 'identity' directs attention towards at least three distinct issues that get tangled under its supremely potent and attractive inscription. These are solidarity, sameness and subjectivity. All of them are engaged in the contemporary practice of black live art, where racialised self-creation is staged and questioned so that interpretive communities and dissident consciousness might be produced.

It took a long time for the disreputable creativity of black artists to climb down from the plinth of primitivism and natural spontaneity and win a different status as modern art. Its initial public codes were created under the protection of the church, where the boundaries of possibility were fixed by the axes of revolutionary hope and conservative quietude. That counter-culture was energised by the momentum of economic development, by the subversive instability of creolisation and by the distinctive liberationist aspirations of ex-slaves, for whom auto-poiesis through labour was not an attractive means to acquire the autonomy for which they yearned. The wild style forged in the heat of slavery leaked out of sacred public space and established its secret and defensive public circles elsewhere. Retaining much of the same formal structure but deploying it towards different ends, the same patterns appeared in the secularised urban world of the nominally free, and founded the unsentimental folk forms of urban workers who were immiserated and poor[7]. From there, it would only be a small step into the profane interior of what would eventually become known as popular culture.

The combination of pleasure and danger that this modern alterity offered to a growing legion of white spectators and mimics was especially appreciated. Black culture's commercial and even aesthetic triumphs were not incompatible with racist assumptions, far from it, though the imperial scripts of hierarchy and absolute difference had to be re-written in some unprecedented forms in order to account for them. The institutional order of white supremacy remained unstable and demanded, as a condition of its continuance, that the grand narrative of racial domination be ritually re-enacted. Minstrelsy, originally a radical form, was reconfigured to meet this obligation. Here the

'... to be real'
The dissident forms
of black expressive
culture

Paul Gilroy

People cannot simply recover the skills and strategies of non-European, pre-colonial and supposedly pure cultural habits and styles that have been erased and changed by decades of displacement and relocation.

supple, exemplary figure of that great black European Josephine Baker (Picasso's 'Nefertiti of now') stands as a reminder of how the ecstasy and spontaneity of a child-like primitive could collude with and then betray the precious dreams of artistic integrity. We know that a whole host of self-conscious modernisms found a place of dubious honour where the uncorrupted spirit of savagery might be contained, venerated and even simulated in the grim rituals that James Clifford has dubbed 'escapist exoticism'[8].

By these and other even more unlikely routes the dis-organic exigencies of colonial social life passed over into the chaotic flux of the post-decolonisation world. New subcultures and counter-cultures - their debts to black forms protruding through the striated surface of disavowal - annexed the metropolitan lives of formerly imperial subjects and their not-so-imperial children. Under the festive and carnal banners of youth, the disaffected offspring of the host community discovered their own strange connections to the greatness of Empire and its subsequent traumatic loss. The Union Jack is opposed by the polychromatic union jill, while dreadlocks become emblematic of a different pastoral dissidence hounded all the way from ancient Stonehenge to the besieged borders of Wanstonia. The underground sound track of gay black Chicago is transposed into the insubordinate rhythm of brit-techno and its mutant vernacular offshoots. The pedagogy of rap finds an austere echo in the serious work of Fun Da Mental, Kaliphz and Cornershop. The hermetic power of dub calls out and generates a ludic reply in the three tone experiments of inter-cultural Midlanders like Bally Sagoo. Jungle has given black London a genre equivalent in stature to its cousins ragga and hip hop.

Fragments of the colonial habitus passed over into the mainstream largely unnoticed by the cultural industries which circulated the commodities that facilitated their spread. These traces of blackness besmirched the clean monumental edifice of white supremacy. They were soon being (dis)articulated in class-specific and generationally-coded forms, in an irreversible process of increase and growth. Their potency was consolidated by a capacity to afford new ways of comprehending gender differences and sexualities. As the century of the colour line draws to a close, they have become part of what it means to be British and they may soon be part of what it means to be a twenty-first century European. Forced intercontinental migration was followed by urbanisation and further,

The desire to affirm and celebrate unbroken continuity is clearly a response to racisms that deny any historical currency to black life.

this time voluntary, long-distance travel. The debris of Britain's decline provided a new setting for the reinvention of the combative, itinerant spirit of marginal modernity and its hybrid modernisms.

The restless creativity celebrated and practiced in this non-traditional modern tradition involves both building and re-building, discovery and memory. People cannot simply recover the skills and strategies of non-European, pre-colonial and supposedly pure cultural habits and styles that have been erased and changed by decades of displacement and relocation. This simple realisation has made the status of origins and survivals, and the legitimacy of creative rediscovery, important issues in post-colonial and black vernacular cultural criticism. Operating by default in the temporality of subordination, and mesmerised by the glamour of white supremacy, too much has rested on the varieties of axiological authority that only duration and continuity can supposedly supply. The imagined and sanctified Africas, used to reinstate simple racial dualism in place of an asymmetrical and unfinished political narrative, are not always compatible with the potent residues of Africa's past, let alone the geo-political agenda set by contemporary Africa. This is not the only setting in which distinctive traditional forms of art and culture become political ciphers of authenticity and legitimacy in a larger conflict that would undermine the aesthetic as a self-contained and self-regulating kingdom. Cultural politics is terminated when culture is exclusively prized for its capacity to remain inert and static. The desire to affirm and celebrate unbroken continuity is clearly a response to racisms that deny any historical currency to black life.

However, that same continuity and the notions of time, civilisation, nationality and ethnicity to which it is irretrievably bound are a poisoned chalice, seductively presented by the very order of power which subaltern cultures, routed from slavery and anti-colonial action, promise to abolish. The neo-nationalist discourse of absolute difference, anteriority and purity merely defers the uncomfortable and inevitable encounter with the white power with which it is wholly, though covertly, complicit.

The idea of Diaspora provides some refuge from the incipient fascisms secreted inside this grim package. Diaspora complements the antiphonic imaginary of the subaltern

'... to be real'
The dissident forms
of black expressive
culture

Paul Gilroy

public sphere. Its cross-cultural poetics allows for a complex conception of sameness and an idea of solidarity that does not repress the differences within in order to maximise the differences between one 'essential' community and others. Diaspora's discomfort with carelessly over-integrated notions of culture, and its rather fissured sense of particularity, fit readily with the best moods of politicised postmodernism which shares an interest in understanding the self as contingently and perfomatively produced. Diaspora accentuates *becoming* rather than *being* and identity conceived diasporically, along these lines, resists reification. Foregrounding the tensions around origins and essences that Diaspora brings into focus, allows us to perceive that identity should not be fossilised or venerated in keeping with the holy spirit of ethnic absolutism. Identity too becomes a noun of process and it is placed on ceaseless trial. Its almost infinite openness provides a timely alternative to the authoritarian implications of mechanical - clockwork - solidarity based on outmoded notions of 'race'[9].

The history of these subaltern political cultures' tangled associations with the rise, consolidation and gradual globalisation of the cultural industries is directly relevant to the concerns of this volume. It is also germane to the history of diaspora identifications promoted by the commodification and eventual planetary circulation of post-slave expressive cultures. To simply repeat those narratives here would do an injustice to the important artists and performers whose work will never be offered for sale in the official circuits. Where the commitment to performance values, techniques and aesthetics are strongest, the assertion of real time resists the processes of reduction and commodification on which the globalised meta-market relies. Even when it shelters in the cobwebbed corners of the avant garde, performance culture struggles against the omnipotence of the cultural industries. It asserts the inviolable integrity of face-to-face interaction and challenges the hyper-reality of pseudo-performance, which is the dominant genre through which the seductive power of these valuable commodities unfolds. Immediacy and proximity re-emerge as ethically charged features of social interaction.

Conflict between itinerant cultures and the logic of commodification that sought to capture, domesticate and even reconstruct them wherever necessary should be acknowledged here even if it cannot be elaborated. The history of black music's battles against the official forms in which it could be frozen and sold, within and beyond the market defined by racial solidarities, is a familiar one but it is nonetheless an important cautionary tale. This is a history which should not just rehearse the heroic triumph of music, or expose the tragic erasure of revolutionary and utopian political sensibilities by the corrosive logic of capital and its adjunct, the evasive leviathan of white supremacy. Evan Eisenberg has made a welcome start in writing an account of the phonograph's impact upon the phenomenology of aural perception[10]. However, the relationship between technology, commodification and the counter-cultural creativity of black performers is seldom addressed in the necessary detail. We must ponder the relationship between hip hop, digital recording technologies, the CD format and the unevenly developed de-skilling and de-valuing of 'auratic'[11] instrumental competence.

The hip hop nation has confined its loudly trumpeted enthusiasm for improvisation within strict limits. Most of the time its favoured mode of reality is a virtual one in which only the illusion of spontaneity is created and the balance between rehearsed and improvised elements of the creative event shifts decisively towards the former. That hip hop is more usually studio rather than stage music and that it is most fully realised in conjunction with video images is conveyed by its obvious disinterest in live recordings and contempt for the input of performing musicians. To note this is not to deny it the status of music, to undermine its own creative possibilities or to suggest that those who apply its formulae lack imagination or technical skill. The difference between sampling a break that someone else created and playing a break of your own in the living collusive circle of an audience that comprehends its dynamics should not however be minimised or denied. It is also possible to acknowledge that disengagement from the instrumental aspects of musical performance has fostered innovative approaches to the staging of hip hop, in which the video cues originally used to sell the music on cable TV have been reproduced in concert settings[12]. The rap show is the decaying half-life of its own video incarnation.

The simple fact that hip hop has been made by performers without instruments prompts a different relationship to music and the dramaturgy of its 'live' shows. The role of

'... to be real'   Paul Gilroy
The dissident forms
of black expressive
culture

**Chila Kumari Burman
and Magic Burman**
Ice Cream and Magic
ICA, London (1994)
Photos: Robert Taylor

'... to be real'   Paul Gilroy
The dissident forms
of black expressive
culture

costumes and props in establishing the visibility of Grandmaster Flash and the Furious Five and of stunts like the synchronised military drill of S1W in securing a memorable profile for Public Enemy are significant staging posts in the sequence that leads to the theatrical sophistication of Ice Cube's recent shows. To say that these melodramatic devices develop or enhance the specifically musical elements of the performance would be laughable. Nobody suggested this when cornball MC Danny Ray led James Brown off the stage in a satin cape or when Alexander O'Neal rolled his famous four-poster onto the stage. It is more interesting to explore how this variety of spectacle establishes the authority of authenticity that the pageants of realness confer.

We should at least consider the possibility that the power of music is itself being undermined in the very gestures that supposedly enhance it. What is fascinating is that even when the musical soundtrack for a live show has been pre-recorded on DAT, the pretence of improvisation and spontaneity has had - for now at least - to be maintained. Public Enemy's Chuck D did not argue when asked by one recent interviewer why 'most hip hop bands are so bad live'. Exempting himself, he made this diagnosis: 'Today you have guys who make a video and never appear live; it's two-dimensional'[13]. There is more to this pattern than corporate pressure to cut down the costs of touring.

In making sense of these developments, we would do well to recall James Brown's epic struggle to win his indifferent record label to the idea that issuing a live recording might be a worthwhile innovation and a valid commercial proposition. We might also occasionally listen to the uncanny intimacy of unedited recordings made in the interlude between Brown's revolutionary leap and the fateful point where the obligation to purge all mistakes and any local ambience took hold. Records like Curtis Mayfield's *Curtis/Live!*[14] might be used to explore these matters as well as the ethical and political value of the performance event in the context of a dynamic social movement which contrasts so sharply with the individualist moods of our own era. These days, the political language of racial solidarity appears not as a sign of democracy yet to come but as one more ephemeral element in the opportunistic marketing of the blessed merchandise that can alone fill out the hollow core of black identity. Nike and Spike Lee, Cross Colours, Karl Kani, Russell Simmons and recently Chuck D himself with his label *Rapstyle* have all striven to fulfil this increasingly desperate need. Now it is the clothed rather than the unclothed body that supplies the visual signatures of the authentic black self.

It would appear that the values of performance stand opposed to those celebrated as performativity: the discursive mode by which ontological effects are conjured into being. Assessing the role of filmed pseudo-performances in orchestrating the cross-over successes of the immortal Bob Marley might supplement this line of enquiry and even shift it in a more cynical, unhomely direction. Taken together, these inter-connected examples remind us that the precious immediacy of live art can serve various ends. If we are to understand what we are losing when 'auratic' performance is replaced by pseudo-performance we must comprehend the role that musicians played in meshing different communicative codes: kinetic and proxemic as well as musical (though not always linguistic) and in establishing the customary principles that for so long governed the management of the authenticity effects common to a medley of different performance genres and creative disciplines. Cheryl Lynn's cry 'to be real' remains the clarion call of sub-sub-cultures but we must ask whether the musicians' authority has now been terminally broken and their historic tactics repudiated by the comprehensive dominance of video and visuality. If music no longer supplies the master signifiers of black creativity, sound and hearing have been supplanted by eyes and visuality. They produce different subjects differently and another, untempered and untested sameness. Their awakening of desire and their soliciting of identification promise the abolition of the old projects of racial solidarity for which sound and orature supplied the keys. Perhaps the contemporary enthusiasm for live art in a variety of dissimilar settings resists this tendency as well as this historic conclusion?

To be inauthentic is sometimes the best way to be real. The illusion of community created by antediluvian musical rituals was all the more powerful as a cultural code because it was recognised as a pretence in which audience and artist could collaborate[15]. A performance emerged from the sum of their combined inputs in circumstances where artists were prepared to take responsibility for the occurrence and the audience to bear witness to the fragile truth of beleaguered black sociality in a relationship that approached

'... to be real'   Paul Gilroy
The dissident forms
of black expressive
culture

mutual accountability. To recall this possibility is neither anachronistic nor sentimental.

Today, class and power, money, gender and sexuality all intervene in the relationship between respectable black live art practice and the lowly vernacular forms which established the prized authenticity effects and the anti-aesthetic codes that enabled the evaluation of all sorts of creative practice. The discrete institutional settings for say, a Bill T Jones dancework, a performance piece by Chila Kumari Burman and a General Levy concert are clearly incompatible. The differences matter but so do the convergences, correspondences and intersections: uncommodifiable real time and real bodies, antiphony, drama and release in the circle of the dance, even when the dancing has stopped and the reasoning has started.

The flourishing of contemporary black performance culture encompasses diverse elements and performance 'disciplines' based in incompatible institutional homes. It has evolved in a complex pattern that systematically confounds the boundaries that have been placed between high and low, vernacular and refined, respectable and disreputable. It also breaks the barriers that exist between different performance media, each comfortably settled in its own fortified domain, regulated by its own caste of specialists, experts and critics and policed by its gate-keepers, regulators of the aesthetic and technical codes that define theatre, music, dance and performance art based on the visual. Where funding is an issue these headings and the gaps between them matter a lot. Where ethico-political fidelity to the counter power that drives black history takes priority, the label under which a creative activity is legitimated is not so important. The unexpected success of underground productions ranging from conventional 'theatrical' shows like *Black Heroes in the Hall of Fame* and *Boops*, to the historic genre-crossing of *Raggamuffin* by Double Edge Theatre Company, testifies to the resilience of performance values.

The appeal of this work in a black vernacular based increasingly on video and visuality is something that deserves much more serious and detailed analysis than can be provided here. Live art practices based in the institutions of the official world of art and culture were not sealed off from the effects of the expressive revolution initiated by *Ragamuffin*.

This theatrical resurgence in the late 1980s was closely connected to the rise of black comedy which has recently superseded it. That scene, with its own modest network of performances spaces and nascent stars - Leo X Chester, Felix Dexter and the rest - is certainly linked to a new stage in the unfolding of self-conscious community. It draws much of its energy and its authority from the intimacy and indubitably moral force of real time and face-to-face interaction between performer and crowd. Black Britons and others who for good reasons may resist the pleasures of that impossible identity have been bonded by the need to laugh at ourselves and our predicament as well as the urge to find different public spaces where the limits of any emergent community might be produced, tested out and worked upon[16]. This activity has been inspired by the rise of Lenny Henry and a proliferation of American imports pirated on video as much as the dubious desire to remain faithful to the anti-modern spirit of African orality.

The ancient power of Eshu and other trickster figures, and the subversive philosophical priorities mandated by the cosmic power of Ashe may indeed have been implicated in the growth of pirate radio. Whatever its inspiration, the invisible reach of radio was the decisive factor in creating minor institutions of publicity. In conjunction with an expansion of the printed sub-culture, radio created a new understanding of community and a different sense of solidarity figured, above all, through the need to protect and develop an expressive culture that was felt to be in jeopardy. However quickly it sold out, crossed over in search of big money or reverted to blackface Thacherite type from its temporary ghettocentric forms, illegal radio was the catalyst for the spectacular consolidation and expansion of a distinct black public sphere. That space of public opinion, disagreement and edutainment would make community palpable in the old antiphonic rituals created around new live performance events. Radio summoned up and delivered an untapped audience. *Black Heroes* moved briefly into the West End and the same route led on into TV land, where commissioners were hungry for minoritarian spice to make their bland fare more interesting. The *291 Club* - the main affirmation of vernacular vitality where the audience is always the biggest star - appeared on the back of local enthusiasm for the talent contest beamed over from the Apollo in Harlem.

The convergences between artists in various creative spheres are not just symptomatic

'... to be real'
The dissident forms
of black expressive
culture

Paul Gilroy

consequences of their common ethnic proclivities. Whether they are conscious of it or not, it would be foolish to deny that these changes are also connected by some common subscription to the licence which ludic post-modernism provides to roam, borrow and transgress. And yet, the power of performance and the need to which it speaks is more than the work of po-mo ventriloquism. Though real time live art shares much of the film-maker's desire to re-invent and re-present the world along different frequencies of sensibility, it is a cultural style that reacts against the capital and labour intensive world of film which has been moved into the centre of our reckoning by the triumphs of the black independent sector in this country and abroad. In all the face-to-face areas, the basic patterns created around the use of music are combined with other registers of communication. They are harnessed but not forgotten. Where performance cultures have passed over the threshold into the space where visuality dominates, there is an unavoidable sense of loss, not because the artists involved lack the means to make the transition but because the collaborative input of their circular audiences cannot be adequately communicated. Without their active witnessing no performance can take place.

1   Robert Farris Thompson, *Flash Of The Spirit: African & Afro-American Art & Philosophy* (Vintage, New York 1984)

2   'Running a Thousand Miles for Freedom: or, The Escape of William and Ellen Craft from Slavery' in *Great Slave Narratives* , ed. Arna Bontemps (Beacon, Boston 1969)

3   Eric Lott, *Love and Theft: Blackface Minstrelsy and the American Working Class* (Oxford 1993). W T Lhamon Jr, *Deliberate Speed* (Smithsonian Institution Press, Washington 1990)

4   Ice T with Heidi Sigmund *The Ice Opinion* (St Martin's Press, New York 1994)

5   Paul Lawrence Dunbar, *Lyrics of Lowly Life* (Dodd Mead, New York 1896)

6   'Gender as Performance', an interview with Judith Butler in Radical Philosophy 67 (Summer 1994)

7   Recent works that address these issues in a variety of histories and locations are: Jon Michael Spencer, *Blues And Evil* (University Press of Tennessee 1993), Carolyn Cooper, '"Me know no law, me know no sin": transgressive identities and the voice of innocence: the historical context' in *Noises In The Blood: Orality, Gender and the 'Vulgar' Body of Jamaican Popular Culture* (Macmillan Caribbean, 1993), Peter Wade, *Blackness and Race Mixture; The Dynamics of Racial Identity In Colombia* (Johns Hopkins University Press, 1993, especially chapter five)

8   James Clifford, 'Negrophilia' in Denis Hollier (ed) *The New History of French Literature* (Harvard University Press 1989)

9   I see strong affinities here with the argument outlined by Rosi Braidotti in 'Sexual Difference as a Nomadic Political Project' in her *Nomadic Subjects* (Columbia University Press, 1994)

10 Evan Eisenberg, *The Recording Angel* (Picador, London 1987)

11 I am thinking of Walter Benjamin's discussion of the work of art's aura and its loss in the era of reproducible cultural artefacts: 'The Work of Art In The Age of Mechanical Reproduction' in *Illuminations,* ed H. Arendt (Fontana, London 1973)

12 Lloyd Bradley, 'Message in a box' in The Guardian, August 30th, 1994, London

13 The Face, August 1994, London

14 Buddah Records, 2659 004, 1971

15 Christopher Small, *Music of the Common Tongue* (John Calder, London 1987)

16 See Langston Hughes, 'Jokes Negroes Tell on Themselves' in Negro Digest, Vol. 9, No.8, June 1951, reprinted in *Mother Wit From The Laughing Barrel,* ed. Alan Dundes (Prentice Hall, New York 1973)

Shishir Kurup
in *Assimilation*
by Raven Group (1991)
Photo: Robert Taylor

IN BETWEEN SPACE
Shishir Kurup

One

My 'people' hail from the southernmost Indian state of Kerala. I, however, was born in Bombay, then raised in Mombassa, Kenya and came of age in the United States of America. Consequently I call myself an Indo-African-American and have been the *other* from the day I was born.

Africa Mother of us all. Black. White. Yellow. Brown.
East Africa. Olduvai Gorge. Possible birthplace of mankind.
Kenya. Land of Masai, Kikuyu and Bantu. Land of red elephants.

Mombassa. Third leg of a thriving trade triangle between Africa, Arabia and India. Mombassa. Ancient port. Sailors been coming here since the dawn of recorded history. Mombassa. Called the island of 'spice and sin' since before Christ blessed the cheesemakers. Mombassa. Arab dhows, not unlike Chinese junks, brought frankincense, myrrh and silk and left with gold, ivory and later slaves. Mombassa. Dhows still come today but with more benign cargo. You can see them bobbing on the ocean as you cross Nyali Bridge like some sort of Douglas Fairbanks wet dream. Mombassa.

Two

I'm a city boy, always have been always will be, in the hustle and bustle of this sleepy little cosmopolis; like a mini New York without the big buildings. We got Arabs and Indians and Africans and Europeans, Hindus and Muslims and Christians and Jews, all hawking their goods and spitting their spit.

The traffic signs read *keep left, keep left,* British style with Peugeots and Fiats and Ford

Anglias. Everyone wants a Chevy Impala because it's American. American is in. Bigger, better. Drive your Chevy down Kilindini Road. We live over here in Pandya House, a tenement building with shops and offices below. Over here is the Regal Cinema which exclusively plays American shoot-em-ups, Italian spaghetti-shoot-em-ups and Chinese Kung-Fu-em-ups. Sam Pekinpah, Sergio Leone, Run-Run Shaw, Raymond Chow. Tickets are two shillings and forty cents for rows A-J (which work out at about a quarter in American cash), 3/6 for rows K-Z and 4/8 for the balcony. In this theatre Eastwood is badass, McQueen is cool, Bronson is tough and Bruce Lee can kick all their asses. Shane and Shaft and Super-Fly and Cleopatra Jones. We hear names like Thalmas Rasulala and Lee Van Cleef. Eli Wallach is the Ugly, Yul Brynner the King and I the kid with the open mouth stuffing popcorn down my throat. In the Indian film houses, Rajesh Khanna, 'Shotgun' Sinha, Dharmendra, reign supreme. Amithab Bachan isn't quite the god he is soon to become and Zeenat Aman is the babe of all our nocturnal emissions.

Next door we have the Husseini Stationery Mart where we get comic books from Britain. Dandy, Beano, Topper and Beezer. And once a year the annuals; real glossy, hardcover versions of these comics. Beano is the most irreverent of the lot, where all that pent-up British repression comes out in cartoon characters like The Bash Street Kids, who never get out of Standard 2B, and Dennis the Menace, a psychotic juvenile delinquent with a taste for blood. From America, Spider-Man, The Sub-Mariner and Mighty Thor give us glimpses of what we think is American life, while from India the Chirta Katha comics give us glimpses of what they think Mahabharatha life was like.

Over here we have the Mombassa bar. Sailors from Turkey and Greece come to drink, vomit and fight the Trojan War all over again while the juke box blares till 2am. Songs like *I can see clearly now the rain is gone, I can see all obstacles in my way* and *When I find myself in times of trouble Mother Mary comes to me* and *Oye como va, miritmo bueno pagosar, mulata*. At least that's how my ears bastardise Spanish. Out on the street the vendors roast their cassava and corn or mogo and makai on rusty grills heated by burning wood which fills empty oil-drums. Beggars line the streets, many with leprosy, asking for any change you might be able to spare, while decked-out Hindu and Muslim women head to their respective places of worship or open bazaars. In April the East African Safari will roar through these streets when some of the world's greatest racing car drivers - like Shekhar Metha, and Joghinder Singh with his tee nee na na tee nee na na car horn - will compete in one of the most gruelling 5,000 kilometre races, which will take them through mountains and plains, jungles and cities. But I won't be there to see it this year. I'm on my way to America.

The immigrant is, as Webster's defines it, 1) one who comes into a foreign country to take up permanent residence there, or 2) a plant or animal that becomes established where it was previously unknown. Establishing this is much simpler in definition than in practice and, curiously enough, is more easily afforded to plants and animals than it is to humans.

This *otherness* is the driving force behind the work I do as an artist. Being an immigrant of my generation has been a catalyst for two solo performance pieces - *Assimilation*, and *EXILE: Ruminations on a Reluctant Martyr* (created in collaboration with Page Leong, Co-artistic Director of our performance collective, Raven Group) - and for *Ghurba*, a play I wrote for the 1993 Los Angeles Festival. *Ghurba*, commissioned by Cornerstone Theater Company, dealt with stories from the Arab-American culture.

Flashback. But first, back to an earlier time. Back to a time of child memory. A time of warm Bombay nights when we sleep on terraced rooftops because it's too damn hot to sleep indoors. The moon is huge and full and close enough to reach out and touch. I lie under the twinkle, twinkle little stars, how I wonder... flanked by my mother on one side and my father on the other with just a few grass mats below us and a thin bedsheet for cover.

A few words and images make the only link to the country where I am 'from'. *Jaggivanram Hospital* - where I was born. *Marin Drive and Choupathi* - where we went for seaside walks. *Bhel Puri* - what we ate when we went on these seaside walks. They swirl in my mind like thinly veiled flashes of a past life, bits of memory. An old moviola, flickering faded and yellowing pictures of a past I sometimes doubt existed. Phantom memories connected to the first tastes of particular foods: roasted fresh corn bought off the streets (a practice I would continue while living in Africa); the first taste of bread and strawberry jam (a colonial hangover I suspect); the first taste of Horlicks (hangover

Shishir Kurup
in *Assimilation*
by Raven Group (1991)
Photo: Robert Taylor

again?). I don't remember.

In Bombay, we lived on the fifth floor of the Railway Quarters which was the housing for the nurses of the nearby hospital where my mother was an RN. Along with tastes and words, I, to this day, remember dreams I had as a child of hanging off the ledge of our fifth floor balcony. Hanging on for dear life. These were vivid, panic-inducing dreams that had a startling clarity - the surroundings accurate in everyday detail. Were these dreams the earliest inklings of *otherness*? Of not belonging? I hung on with three-year-old fingers, never quite able to pull myself onto the ledge. Unable to pull myself up or to let go. Unable to do anything but hang there, hoping for the kindness of strangers to haul me up onto a two-foot ledge of safety.

The other. The uprooted. The foreign. Even in Bombay, Keralites were the minority, the ones who had to assimilate, learn the regional language, mask their southernness, their difference. So, the feeling of having to tread softly, of not being on stable ground, of being the outsider looking in, was always present, prominent. The feeling that, at any given moment, any of the legitimate citizenry could say, 'This is not your house, you're only renting. Go back to where you came from.' 'Go back' is misleading. There is no *going back*. At least not for me. My parents' generation talk endlessly about it, but few, if any, really do go back. And this idealised 'home' they're going back to is suspect, because it doesn't really exist anymore.

> *Taleb* (talking to his daughter):
> *I have heard that this house... my house... our house... was torn down soon after we left. It's a strange feeling because in my mind the house still stands; my house still exists and that life carries on like I remember it, but I also know that nothing really stays the same and that change is inevitable. I know it well. Change. It is an unwelcome guest that forces itself on me, my only weapon against it my memory. You see, if it exists in my mind it must exist somewhere in this universe... and so... this home... that I grew up in and will never see again... is still preserved somewhere. In me. In you.* Ghurba

What would make one leave the safety of the familiar to go far away, to alien places? A particular restlessness of spirit? The promise of adventure? Or is it purely financial: to make good, succeed, put food in the childrens' mouths? The struggle to get out and start anew in a new place is so great that odds are you will fight to stay put. Once that's done, a routine is established, a life of certain comfort is achieved, then *going back* becomes even more difficult. So, this dream of returning home is just that: a dream. *Going back* would have to be back in time, because where you are is when you are and who you are.

Indianness. The gulf between Kerala and Bombay may not be the vast ocean between Bombay and Mombassa, or Mombassa and the United States, but is a gulf nonetheless. However, we were unified by our Indianness, even though as Indians very little unified us. Until, that is, we became immigrants in a new world. Then a lot of our differences evaporated into a general recognition of *Indianness*.

I've always boasted that I can 'spot an Indian at fifty paces'. It's true, I can. And they can usually spot me. We actively seek each other out. In shopping malls, restaurants or movie theatres. The knowing smile or nod of the head and the obligatory, 'You're from India? Which part?' We're fascinated with others like us. This gives comfort and creates an illusion that we, perfect strangers, know each other better than we actually do. You seek out comfort in what feels familial but have to accept with it the caveat of conflict.

Purity *(A television flickers on and Gibbo appears. This is Saleem's memory sequence. He interacts with the video image.)*

G   Eh, you dirty bugger. Keep the lines pure, man. Marry an Indian girl.

S   What about love?

G   Love. That'll come. After you're married. First we have to get you a nice Indian girl.

S   I don't want you to.

G   Oh, what are you going to do - marry one of these whities? Man, the women here will leave you like that. It's in their nature. Bugger it man, they don't even wash their arses.

S   Why do you always bring that up?

G Areh baba, speak the truth and shame the devil. Honesty is the best policy. We all know that all they do is wipe with their perfumed toilet paper, dirty buggers.

S You know, I can't think of a woman without thinking about that.

G Good, good. That's the point, a deterrent. Just say no, no. What's the problem? Think only about Indian women. They're clean. Anyway, why do you want one of them - so that you can become more of a saipe than you already are, Uncle Tom?

S Don't call me that.

G What? Saipe? European?

S I am not a saipe nor am I an Uncle Tom.

G Sure, sure. That's what you say. Listen to the way you talk. Like a proper London Bhai. I don't talk like that. I've held on to my culture. They used to make fun of this accent. Not anymore. We'll give them a few, you know? You can't lose your culture, man, that's all you've got. Your community. Remember when we were younger and these whities called you a wog? Who came and gave them good beatings? Hahn? Who helped you? Hahn? Your community, you bastard. Your woggy community. You don't even remember.

S I didn't ask for any help.

G Areh, areh bigshot! Didn't want our help, eh? You like being called a wog, eh?

S I was trying to reason with them.

G Oh, yah, yah, yah. I remember, you standing on the park bench with that massive dictionary.

S The OED

G Yah, the OED, asking them to define "wog." You're a strange bugger you know that, Sala. They would have broken your head in two seconds if we hadn't come and now you're saying all this? What an ungrateful bastard you are. Look, they made us their subjects and then what? They want us to come here and be their coolies again. No thank you Sahib. Not again. Not this time. This time you're going to work for me. And if I have to hit you on the head with a stick a couple of times, that's okay too. It's a matter of survival man.

S   When will we stop surviving and start living?

G   Oh, big, big questions. Why don't you ask your gora friends that? *(beat)* When will we stop surviving and start living. You're a pithy bugger, Ehn? *(beat)* Look man, I don't even want to speak this language of theirs. Soon, I won't. I'll speak only my mother tongue.

S   Then what? I don't speak your mother tongue. I barely speak my own.

G   Don't worry. We'll burn that bridge when we get to it, Uncle Tom. Tommy. Tom-Tom. Tom-Bhai.

(Video Gibbo blips off. Saleem recovers from this encounter by smearing his make-up once across from the black side to the brown. He then reclines, picks up his guitar and plays.)

EXILE: Ruminations on a Reluctant Martyr

Three
Community. The first battle the immigrant has to fight is with his family and community. Community, in this context, is defined by ethnic background and not necessarily affinity. What the community thinks is of great importance to the family. It's the lifeline to the homeland. The salve to the guilt of leaving, of being the lucky ones. The ones who got out. Assimilate, but maintain your cultural ties. Easier said than done. And what does that mean anyway, since there are no formulas or guidelines to measure how much assimilating and how much cultural maintenance is appropriate?

In order to become American you have to be twice as good as Americans... at everything. That's the immigrant's song. Work twice as hard for half as much and make sacrifices. Live for your childrens' future, not yours, and make them pay too. To continue your sacrifice. Pay with their complete subservience to the family unit. The only unit that

Shishir Kurup in *EXILE:
Ruminations on
a Reluctant Martyr*
by Raven Group (1992)
Photo: Robbie Cavolina

matters. It's the Mafia, the Cosa Nostra, the Tong. The need to belong, to make good, the overwhelming desire to put forth your best foot translates into nothing of weakness, all of strength. Strength is what the dominant culture values, which in the United States means financial success and power. Money talks and bullshit walks! That's why there are so many Indian doctors, engineers and nuclear physicists in the US. And so few artists. Money talks and bullshit walks!

The artist. Because the role of the artist is essentially to question existing norms, both within the confines of his family and particular community and outside in the construct of society at large, it puts the family and the community in a position of vulnerability in an increasingly predatory culture. Hopefully the artist responds to these two situations with reflexivity. Since the questions asked tend to be about issues of sexuality, gender roles and overt and internalised racism - in essence the airing of your dirty laundry - the artist becomes a threat. A threat to the family and to the community. A threat to putting your best foot forward. A threat against making good. The threat of exploitation of any perceived weakness. Insularity is survival, candour is death.

Art is the graffiti of the soul, the process of screaming, 'Hey I was here... I'm still here!'

The artist gets in touch with the anger of the immigrant, the anger that is not allowed to rear its ugly head. The anger that could eventually blow up in your face. *Don't bite the land that feeds you.* This is your life now, even if it's killing you to make a living. Become an American at all costs, but live by the rules of the homeland, because even though you despise your inferiority as the *other*, you secretly believe that these people are an uncouth, unclean, immoral, bunch of riff-raff. Better to bottle up what you feel. Survival at all costs. But, as Saleem says in *EXILE*, 'when will we stop surviving and start living?'

I often feel that the dominant culture is playing a game with me in asking me, as an artist, to share my thoughts with them. My fear is that it's all being taken down to be used against me when they decide to withdraw this invitation they have extended. After I, as flavour of the month, have been thoroughly sucked dry. The paranoia of the immigrant! I used to feel that I should learn how to operate all forms of automation so that if the end were in sight I could get away. I call it Mad Maxophobia. Where would I get away to? I don't know. Paranoia of the immigrant!

Paranoia. Plunged into a world so alien my mind is reeling and all I think is, *can I keep floating, bobbing and weaving, as you ask me questions you've no business asking me but I don't know that and I don't dare tell you that because I want to belong. Belong in a place where I am both the curious and the curiosity.* We all know what happened to the cat. Belong in a place where I am Kwai Chang Caine or The Fugitive or The Incredible Hulk, moving from town to town, stopping long enough to raise eyebrows but never threatening. A jack-of-all-trades, slave to none. A shadow-boxer, a phantom, ducking and feinting. Someone you can't lay a glove on, eventually becoming punch-drunk, gun-shy, with tics and no tact. Don't pigeon-hole me, don't think you know me, know how I feel. I know how you feel. I know how you think. I know where you live. I live in your world. I speak your language, but you don't speak mine. That pisses me off and you don't understand why? It's the deep end of the pool man and I'm wet behind the ears, so I listen closely to the dialects and colloquials, the hip-cats, the hep-cats, in like Flynn, the Gentleman Jim. Hit the streets a-runnin' and try to please the masses, go get yourself some cheap sunglasses. 'Hey you sound safe, you can pass. If you master the father tongue you can pass and everything is okay - if you pass.' *Passing.* Like passing a stone you forgot about. Only later you discover the pain. Only later you assess the damage. Only later you mourn what was lost and accept what is gained. Like a bottom feeder, you blend into the rocks 'cause one false move and you could be dead.

Too dramatic? Maybe. But you're reading and I'm spewing.

Language. My mother-tongue is Malayalam, a palindrome. From the day I was born I've never conversed in it as the language of choice. In Bombay, we spoke in Maharati, Hindi and English outside, Malayalam and English at home. In Kenya, we spoke in Gujarati, Hindi, Swahili and English outside, Malayalam and English at home. In the United States, my mother would speak to me in Malayalam and I would retort in English, providing hours of amusement for my school mates. Friends asked me if I thought in other languages and then converted foreign thought into English, or if I dreamt in a foreign tongue. As far as I know the answer to both queries is... no. Although I

I have recently become an American citizen after twenty years of ambivalence. Is it this ambivalence that maintains my otherness, and vice versa? I now have an American passport. Am I now an American? Is that all it takes?

understand Malayalam fully, I have now effectively lost all my adopted languages and am solely an English speaker. It's like a kind of stroke, where I can visualise the words but can't translate into language. What has been lost and what has been gained?

Four

In *EXILE: Ruminations on a Reluctant Martyr* I created a character, an alter ego who was set adrift in a sea of loneliness. A writer trapped by his own words. The set, designed by my collaborator Page Leong, reflected this isolation: a small sofa or love-seat on a three-foot-tall platform in the middle of a darkened space, surrounded by half a dozen six-foot-tall stacks of books, resembling an island in a sea of black with spires erupting from below. From the love-seat, pages of writing explode, with pencils strewn everywhere, words on paper, crumpled and carelessly tossed about. A creature sits on this very messy black island, in a glittering kimono, rumpled shirt and silk boxers, like a house-bound geisha. When the creature is revealed it's face is parti-coloured, creating, essentially, a peace sign with one eye and cheek area painted black. The other eye and cheek area are painted brown, and the mouth and chin area are painted white. I see with a black eye, I see with a brown eye, but I speak with a white mouth. Large scrolls of writing hang on the walls of the space, literalising the feeling of being caged by words. The piece was created as a response to censorship. Censorship from within and without, first inspired by the plight of Salman Rushdie.

Fear. Ever since coming to the United States I have had a feeling of unease that I have never been able to shake. A feeling, that I identified only a few years ago, as fear. It's as if I am running from a bear that stopped chasing me a long time ago, but I'm still running. A feeling that the land under my feet is not stable and could give way at any moment. It's funny that now I live in California: land of bears and shaky ground.

Ambivalence. I have recently become an American citizen after twenty years of ambivalence. Is it this ambivalence that maintains my otherness, and vice versa? I now have an American passport. Am I now an American? Is that all it takes? Or is it something to be taken, vehemently, by force? A vehement voice that isn't necessarily strident or martial, but can be if it chooses to be. A vehement form that isn't necessarily

'What we're looking for is not a caricature of an Indian, what we want is a sort of... Peter Sellars thing, funny but real.'

exclusive but can be if it chooses to be. Vehement content. Vehement form. Using symbols that only 'we' who have lived under your rules understand. Our own code that allows us to communicate in morse. But who is this monolithic 'we'? In the United States, unlike in Britain, the term 'black' is not used to refer to all artists of colour. Each hue is given its appropriate place, and geography defines which one is dominant. In the politics of black and white, I occupy an uneasy position, an in between position, a position where tribalism based on ethnicity is frightening. So Chicano power and black nationalism scare me almost as much as white supremacy. Either way, my ass is grass.

Being caught between spaces has been the constant. The space where I am placed, and ultimately the space where I feel most at home. What is on either side of inbetween? I see it everyday. On television, on screen, in the media. It's not me. Could I ever occupy that space?

Not yet. The little old lady from Iowa 'aint ready for it. She was a slightly chubby round-faced woman in her late forties, and I was there to read for her show. Actually, not her show, but she cast it. Or maybe she was the assistant. *Murder She Wrote*, I think it was, with the grande dame of television mystery, Angela Lansbury. It's amazing what Anglophiles Americans are. Anything with an English sheen is seen as a cut above, cultured, a return to a time when this culture had culture. They disdain the culture right beneath their noses, even as it influences their kids and slowly seeps into the mainstream consciousness. Even though salsa has replaced tomato ketchup as the condiment of choice. They disdain the smells of all the different ethnic stews brewing and percolating and slowly spilling out, adding spice to this meat-and-potatoes land. They disdain the fact that a new American race is being born that is a mix of black, white, brown and yellow, and it is something to behold.

Anyway, I had come in to audition for the part of an Indian something or another. The usual roles available to me, in Hollywood, are either the heavily accented, turbaned, 7-11 Quick Mart counter clerk or the dusky, black and white khuffiyah-wearing terrorist with that generic middle-eastern accent. The occasional doctor pops up, but not all that often, and always heavily accented. These cartoons are usually characters to be reviled or the butt of the joke (the joke usually being the accent). So, the casting woman, by way of answering my concerns about stereotypes, said, 'What we're looking for is not a caricature of an Indian, what we want is a sort of... Peter Sellars thing, funny but real.' It was the only image of Indians from which she had to draw.

Internalised racism. After I put back the jaw I dropped on the casting office floor, I recalled laughing uproariously with my mother at *The Party*, the Peter Sellars film to which this woman was referring. I had often defended the film as being okay because Sellars was the hero and, bumbling as he was, he wasn't the butt of the joke, although some of the funniest sequences dealt with his very Indian pronunciation of 'Birdie, num, num'. This always sat uneasily with me. I had grown up with Indians making fun of other Indians who they felt didn't speak English as well as they were supposed to, in essence identifying with the oppressor. The rage right now on the *Def Jam Comedy Hour* is for black people to get on stage and 'snap' at other black people, many of the put-downs starting with, 'Your mother's so black...' Indian women have been putting cuticura powder on their face to be 'more fair', and as a child I was made to put on powder whenever I left the house: wouldn't want to be seen looking too dark. So a lot of my solo performances have dealt with the issues of internalising this feeling of *feeling less than*. Is this a link to the high rate of black-on-black shootings in this the land of the free?

In Milwaukee
Hole-in-the-wall Thai place. Siam.
Great food. Motherly waitress. Dahng.
Married to German-American Kluss. So, Dahng Kluss.
Spicy food. Warm human being. Comfort to my frozen tropical ass out of place in that Lake Michigan bone-cutting chill.
Reminiscent of my mother's South Indian chow.
Reminiscent of my mother.
Dahng's eight-year-old Susie. Beautiful child. Love-of-her-life.
Really her niece but adopted and brought here to have a better life as American.
This day I enter Siam
leaving the howling windy street to the warmth of Dahng's
'Come in, come in. Sit down, sit down. It cold outside, huh?

You cold, huh? Want some spicy shrimp? Spicy shrimp and rice?
It good! Hot! Warm you up. Good for you. I know, I know. No MSG.'
Our usual introductory ritual.

Today, however, her warmth was tempered by a sadness in her eyes.
'What's the matter Dahng?'
'Oh...you know my Susie?'
'Yeah.'
'She come home today. She crying. She say her friends call her a chink. I say, you not
a chink, you not a chink.'

Then she told me a story of when Susie was five.
Time for her to become a citizen.
The child is taken to the naturalisation office to be sworn in.
When the ceremony is complete and the oath of allegiance taken the judge leans over
and says to the five-year-old
'Susie you're now an American.'
The child looks back and says, 'When I get my blue eyes?'

Dahng said, 'You know, when I hear that, my tear wanna fall down.'

Assimilation

Five

Cornerstone Theater Company. In July 1993 I started working on a piece for
Cornerstone Theater Company, a group of artists committed to working in disparate
communities and adapting classical or creating new texts for the issues and concerns of
the communities involved. For six years they travelled the highways and byways of rural
America, pulling into small towns and setting up in local halls, school houses or barns,
which were donated by the various chambers of commerce for the specific reason of
putting on a play. They would then go about auditioning the townfolks, most of whom
had never seen a play let alone been in one, casting them alongside the professional
actors of the core ensemble. In 1992 the company came to Los Angeles to begin urban

**Raven Group with
Cornerstone Theater
Company, *Ghurba* (1993)**
Photos: Lynn Jeffries

Raven Group with
Cornerstone Theater
Company, *Ghurba* (1993)
Photos: Lynn Jeffries

residency work, since it is fairly common knowledge that the largest concentration of any particular ethnic group outside of its respective native country exists here, providing the most opportune chance to explore the true nature of that buzz-word-turned-anathema, *multi-culturalism*. What exists here, however, is tribalism. Insular communities that rarely, if ever, go beyond the borders of their turf. Therein lay the challenge.

Ghurba is an Arabic word which means *longing for home and/or estrangement*. Our work on the piece began with interviews with Arab-Americans city-wide. These were both inter-generational and inter-cultural. Our core ensemble, which consisted of Arab-American actors, Cornerstone and Raven Group company members, interviewed Los Angeles Arabs whose backgrounds ranged from Morocco to Iraq. We asked them about their experience of emigrating and acculturating and assimilating. The first thing we discovered was that there is no such thing as a monolithic Arab-American community, especially one defined by geography like so many others. But there is Arab culture. The bond is the Arabic language, but only in its classical form. Just like the first wave of Indian-Americans that came here, Arabs assimilated thoroughly and became 'model minorities', a term often used to describe Asian-Americans. Consistently maligned in the media, they have become far more vocal and far less model about this mistreatment. (Witness the changing of certain offensive lyrics in Disney's recent *Aladdin*.) It is still, however, open season on Arabs in Hollywood. (Witness their treatment in the aptly titled *True Lies*, by the antichrist duo of James Cameron and Arnold Schwarzenegger.)

While the interviews were being conducted, the core and I auditioned and cast seven more members to add to the company, several of whom, in true Cornerstone tradition, had never been on stage before. The ages of the cast ranged from 12 to 72. Finally, the entire cast was interviewed so that bits of everyone's lives would somehow resonate in the piece. I was interested in telling a completely different American story. That of the new immigrant. To my knowledge this was the first piece dealing with these particular issues involving Arab-Americans that had ever been produced in America.

The story that evolved out of the interview experience, with the influence of Edward Said's book, *After the Last Sky*, was a simple one in which the notion of ghurba was concretised into a place. A kind of promised land towards which disparate travellers journey.

Six

Having now become a mutable creature, I recognise that, as a survival tactic, I am slowly coming to understand the repercussions of being in a constantly reactive state. But this frenzy for survival has also, ultimately, made me the artistic hyphenate that I am. Actor-writer-director-musician. Indo-African-American. As I struggle with issues of identity in a society that barely recognises me, I can take comfort in the community I have found at the fringes of the Los Angeles arts basin and in the tribes to which I have consented to belong, namely Cornerstone and Raven Group. Not because of my skin colour, or my accent, or my ethnicity, but because of affinity.

I still hang off the ledge in three-year-old dreams, but as the years have passed, the fear has diminished in commensuration with the amount of time passed, and the amount of comfort of sharing the fight with others.

With thanks to Page Leong.

54

Keep on running
The politics of black
British performance

Catherine Ugwu

KEEP ON RUNNING
The politics of black British performance

Catherine Ugwu

> I would go so far as to claim that a new kind of cultural
> worker is in the making, associated with a new politics of
> difference. *Cornel West*[1]

Struggles around difference and the appearance of new identities in political and artistic arenas have provoked powerful challenges to the dominant narratives of the modern world. One such challenge - live art - embraces a broad church of overlapping and shifting aesthetics, ideologies and methods of production. Live art's very resistance to categorisation and containment, and its ability to surprise and unnerve, makes its impact far-reaching. Growing numbers of black artists are engaging in live art practice, viewing it as one of the few remaining spaces available to express complex ideas of identity.

Conceptual in nature, the work is invariably driven more by the expression of ideas than the desire to display skills. Subverting tradition and defying convention, live art invokes different ways of seeing, thinking and doing. With no fixed form, materials or genre, this area of practice offers artists the opportunity to select from traditional and contemporary cultural influences, references and icons - from carnival to disco, from past to present.

The cultural outpourings of black British 'communities' exhibit an amalgamation of African, Asian, Caribbean, South East Asian, European and American influences, reflecting the hybrid experience of our constant movement between very distinct worlds. Black artists working in the area of live art engage with this form because it allows them the unruly polyvocality required to represent a difference that hints at what is formative not of nations but of both individual and society. This hybrid culture is a manifestation

Live art's very resistance to categorisation and containment, and its ability to surprise and unnerve, makes its impact far-reaching. Growing numbers of black artists are engaging in live art practice, viewing it as one of the few remaining spaces available to express complex ideas of identity.

We are currently witnessing the emergence of an energetic, forceful and politicised generation of black live artists who are breaking new ground in the articulation of the experience of a black community in crisis in Britain.

56

Keep on running
The politics of black
British performance

Catherine Ugwu

of the crisis of alienation and fragmentation being felt across a number of black British communities. Uncertainty and anxiety, fuelled by persistent racism and the increasing disenfranchisement of the black community, goes hand in hand with the realisation that legal equity does not automatically translate into political, social and economic equality. This, coupled with the rise of the radical right and the changing meaning of 'race' itself, has resulted in direct attacks on the notion that some kind of homogenous essentialised black culture exists, is achievable or advantageous. This shift in focus necessitates that we embrace and examine the diversity of the black experience and look to a future which has a new hybrid culture at its heart.

> In a world in which everyone's identity has been thrown into question, the mixing and fusion of disparate elements to create new, hybridised identities point to ways of surviving, and thriving, in conditions of crisis and transition. *Kobena Mercer*[2]

We are currently witnessing the emergence of an energetic, forceful and politicised generation of black live artists who are breaking new ground in the articulation of the experience of a black community in crisis in Britain. Their commitment to investigating individual identity does not necessarily negate an understanding and commitment to selective communally-oriented inter-cultural battles, acknowledging their power within certain arenas and on particular issues. But group-oriented oppositional positions, which negate the specificity of individual experience, which feed into essentialised notions of black and limit the scope of individual artistic expression, have been abandoned by some artists, rejected as received black responses to racism that inadvertently accommodate white agendas - agendas which aimed to support and sustain the position of oppressed and oppressor by employing strategies which mirror the colonisation process.

The invisibility of black artists and their work, coupled with the general expectation that the work of black artists, when visible, may in one way or another be characteristic of a universal black experience, or only communicate with the marginalised community from which it comes, has been detrimental. Collectively, these preconceptions and presumptions have inevitably limited representation of the diversity of the black experience and confirmed established misconceptions of the 'other'. The most inspired work challenges these assumptions.

One of the difficulties in writing this paper - and a recurrent frustration which can be applied generally to the whole area of live art practice - is the impossibility of tracing the histories of its evolution. This is due to a combination of factors. Live art practice works in opposition to any notion or possibility of commodification: it actively seeks to produce ephemeral experiences rather than 'objects', experiences which live in the imaginations and memories of its viewers. As a result, even the most expressive, detailed and varied forms of documentation have failed to capture the essence of the work.

Many factors have contributed to the invisibility of black live artists. The narrow aesthetic interpretations of the 'art world', the exclusion of work from major art institutions, minimal resources and support structures and the relatively few black critics, thinkers and writers embraced by the area have meant that only a handful of black artists are 'officially' associated with the evolution of live art in the UK. For instance, David Medalla's contribution to this area of practice and other art forms over the last thirty years is phenomenal, yet so little information on his work is available.

Between the late 60s and early 70s, Medalla produced a series of *Participation-Production* pieces. These works addressed notions of representation and clearly sought to engage the viewer in a process which encouraged interaction between the artist, the work and themselves.

Each of these participation pieces provided a metaphorical setting and a specific production process for the public to engage with. The three principal works of this type were: *Stitch in Time* (set up in many venues since 1968), a suspended construction of rope, cotton reels and sheets on which people were invited to embroider anything they liked; *Porcelain Wedding* (1973), a ceremony in which, first, a recumbent couple was covered with 'suits' of clay tablets, and then all the participants were invited to make separate clay

58

Keep on running   Catherine Ugwu
The politics of black
British performance

> sculptures referring to the Seven Days of Creation; and
> *Eskimo Carver* (Artists For Democracy, London, 1977), a
> many-levelled performance-exhibition-event in which visitors
> were invited to make 'knives' from a pile of refuse collected
> locally, then to title them and mount them on the walls of the
> gallery in a playful parody of ethnographic museum
> exhibitions. *Guy Brett*[3]

When Isaac Julien adapted his film *Looking For Langston* into a site specific performance piece (staged in both London and Newcastle as part of the 1990 Edge Festival), his concerns included an investigation of sexual and cultural identity, inter-cultural conflict and dialogue, and the historical and contemporary assessment of black cultural expression. The siting of the piece - in Camley Street near Kings Cross station in London - was clearly important and chosen to challenge the preconceptions associated with the area by a range of potential viewers. As Julien points out, it is 'a street that is notorious as a cruising ground for straights'[4] and the choice of location made the issues confronted by the performance more powerful, inducing an immediacy and authenticity often lacking in film or traditional theatre settings.

> I enjoyed the idea of putting my audience into these different
> and difficult spaces where they might not normally go and
> certainly might not feel safe at that time of night. I wanted
> people to go into these spaces and to think about their
> architecture and its relationship to different dynamic forms of
> power - public and private, micro and macro. Making the
> film meant that I could expose those locations cinematically
> but actually putting people - performers and audiences - into
> these landscapes has a different kind of excitement... The
> audience is manoeuvred out of their passive position. They
> can also participate.[5]

Like Julien, Mona Hatoum's early performance work was marked by its provocative,

Isaac Julien
Looking for Langston
Photo: John Kippin/
Locus + Archive
Newcastle-Upon-Tyne

Pamela Sneed
*Imagine Being More
Afraid of Freedom Than
Slavery* (1994)
Photo: Robert Taylor

Elia Arce
*I Have So Many
Stitches That
Sometimes I Dream
That I'm Sick* (1993)
Photo: Martin Cox

60

Keep on running   Catherine Ugwu
The politics of black
British performance

dangerous nature and its ability to take on some complex issues by highlighting the importance of symbolic representation. Utilising various media, including installation, video and performance, she layered meaning to reflect this complexity.

Her live works, produced during the 80s against the backdrop of the civil war in the Lebanon, engaged her in a series of works investigating identity and oppression. These were performances, as Guy Brett has observed, 'in which her own physical presence as a Palestinian women intensified a metaphor of suffering and struggle which could stand for the experience of oppressed peoples in any part of the world'.[6] As Mona Hatoum herself states of performance art, 'the artist is being herself, making her own statement, and not pretending to be someone else, somewhere else.'[7]

The lack of historical documentation, charting the contribution of these and other black artists to the area of live art practice, is a tragic loss to our cultural legacy. Despite this, the last few years have witnessed the emergence of a wide range of exciting performers - artists who want to be heard, want to make their mark, make a difference. Live art provides an arena within which these many voices can co-exist.

Live art entices audiences to challenge established conventions by subverting expectations of order, makes them responsible for their own relationships and response. Cutting edge performance work from both the UK and US is primarily being produced and generated within densely populated, multi-cultural urban communities. These immense, sprawling masses, complex contradictions of diversity in all its forms, exhibit the most fearful signs of our contemporary condition. Live art is crucial to the enforced hybridity of urban existence. It is able to contribute to the process of excavating old worlds and constructing new ones. It engages audiences in cultural encounters which are pertinent to the present.

> Art should not be different from life but an action within it.
> *John Cage*[8]

A substantial amount of the black US performance work recently seen in the UK and much traditional black theatre practice in the UK, has used testimony to frame personal

Page 62
Susan Lewis
Walking Tall (1993)
Photos: Robert Taylor

histories. Informed, particularly in America, by the vocabulary and form of the black religious experience, it accurately captures and conveys through performance the historic relationship between cultural activity and sacred practice. The secularisation which has occurred in recent years within many Western democracies and specifically in the US, has left a space in contemporary black discourse, the far-reaching effects of which are currently being felt.

Testimony is central to the work of many US artists such as The Hittite Empire, Elia Arce, Rhodessa Jones and her work with Cultural Odyssey and the Medea Project, Lynel Gardner, Robbie MaCauley and Pamela Sneed. The process embraced by many of these artists is cathartic. The work attempts to engage both the artist and audience in a process of memorialisation, within which it is hoped some kind of purification will occur.

> I've come to the realisation that we're at a place as a whole culture and society where theatre has evolved as a healing art. I think that's what's happened with performance art, that's what's happened with experimental theatre, that's what's happened with storytelling theatre. *Rhodessa Jones*[9]

Artists need to create a space for a ritual which will highlight the absences in entrenched historical accounts of inequity carried as a result of enslavement. Following in a tradition of African-American autobiography, this work is often an attempt to recreate the fragments of a past amongst a people whom many have dismissed as having no collective history. The public performance and witnessing of personal stories, honouring friends and lovers, family and ancestors allows us to grieve losses, validate our condition and invoke alternative histories which look to a future with hope.

> We tell ourselves our individual stories so as to become aware of our general story. *Ralph Ellison, 'The Invisible Man'*[10]

The history of black British oppression is in some ways similar and yet different from the black American experience. This is occasionally demonstrated in the means of resistance employed by marginalised communities and in the current work of some live artists, on

Keep on running
The politics of black
British performance

Catherine Ugwu

both sides of the Atlantic. The artistic response to inequity embraced by these artists relates to the de-colonisation strategies applied across all areas of cultural production. As Coco Fusco points out, 'Resistance within a colonial context is rarely direct, overt, or literal; rather, it articulates itself through semantic reversals and through the process of infusing icons, objects, and symbols with different meaning... They are among the many ways oppressed people have developed to take their identity back.'[11]

Opposition and resistance has come in a variety of forms, a clear indication of the shrewd ability of the oppressed to be one step ahead. Methods often utilised by oppressed groups globally, embody the reappropriation and redeployment of a range of beliefs, customs and rituals. This has historically provided disengaged groups with the means to reinvent and maintain prohibited marginalised traditions. Caribbean Carnival, and its British equivalent Notting Hill Carnival, exemplify the artistic realisation of this type of resistance and indeed the process by which tradition itself evolves.

Carnival is a well-documented and developed cultural practice across all the islands of the Caribbean. It originated as both a response to the displacement experienced by islanders of African and Asian descent and as a protest to the dominant cultures whose spaces they now shared. Breaking down artform boundaries, it fuses media - including music, dance, costume art and burlesque - to induce unofficial mass experiences which seek to ridicule and undermine the establishment, or sometimes just to entertain. The precise elements which make up carnival are always specific to the political and cultural context within which it happens, making each carnival event unique. It is always engaged with the realities of a particular community and is invariably defiant.

Its refusal to be confined or contained is achieved by its choice of location - siting itself in streets and public spaces. The viewer is always central. It is a communal act of self-expression that is never regulated or controlled by any one artist, everyone is invited to participate: it is this mass audience and artist intervention which creates the spectacle.

The most effective live work is able, in one way or another, to invoke an almost intuitive understanding of the complexity of our various conditions and the circumstances which created them. This work, either directly or indirectly using the artist and his or her life experiences as the starting point, interrogates the racial complexities which are at the foundation of British life.

> Those people who are in western civilisation, who have grown up in it, but yet are not completely a part (made to feel and themselves feeling they are outside) have a unique insight into their society. That, I think, is important - the black man or woman who is born here and grows up here has something special to contribute to western civilisation. He or she will participate in it, see it from birth, but will never be quite completely in it. What such persons have to say, therefore, will give a new vision, a deeper and stronger insight into both western civilisation and the black people in it. *C L R James*[12]

Susan Lewis takes as the starting point for her work her identity as a black woman. Both *Walking Tall* and *Ladies Falling* investigate the many facets of female suppression. Her work is personified by risk and expressive subjectivity. Interest often focuses on the black female body, emphasising its general absence from the contemporary visual discourse by arranging it in compositions of stunning visuality. Both works embody the inner conflict of a woman confronting sexist and racist stereotypes in an effort to replenish her life and actualise her talents. The choice of form for both pieces reflects the alienation and frustration she feels as an artist from conventional practice. Both solo pieces, the works embrace a combination of personal investigation and transformation.

Walking Tall, a movement-based performance piece, draws on the myth of Isis to examine the contemporary black female experience. It captures the process of Lewis embracing her own worth and autonomy as a black woman within a male-dominated and race-beset society. The performance recreates the inner conflicts, history and ambiguities of her life. It challenges outside pressures placed on black women by media images and dominant narratives to match up to Western notions of beauty. Lewis attacks the tendency to internalise this racism by black women, which encourages and sustains anxieties around their physical being, using the culturally specific symbols of hair and

66

Keep on running   Catherine Ugwu
The politics of black
British performance

Susan Lewis
Ladies Falling (1994)
Photo: Robert Taylor

SuAndi
The Story of M **(1994)**
Photo: Robert Taylor

68

Keep on running
The politics of black
British performance

Catherine Ugwu

skin colour to illustrate these points. Her mixed race background motivates her interest in both cultural interweaving and the outdated skin colour hierarchies within the black community.

Ladies Falling traces the historical and current alienation and fragmentation experienced by the black British Diaspora. The work questions our sense of home - whether it is here in Britain or somewhere else - and addresses the complexities of racial and class stratification, history, aesthetic and spiritual development and belonging.

The symbols of tea, sugar and rum are used as metaphors to map out a counter history which discloses the different 'value' of similar objects in differing cultures. Movement, film, costume and gesture are used to symbolise the restricted and repressed nature of established value systems.

Like Susan Lewis, SuAndi provides a unique insight into British society and the diversity of the black British experience. Her performance work - *The Story of M* - confronts the present by excavating the past. *The Story of M* is a narrative text/slide performance, using stories about yesterday to expose the limited ground covered in eradicating racism in all its guises. Set in a hospital ward, SuAndi sits alone in a chair and recounts the life story of her mother, punctuated by a strategically placed, private collection of family photographs and memorabilia.

Witnessing family stories littered with racist encounters, we eventually realise her mother was a working class white women who married a black man, had black children and fought all her life to protect them from the daily inequity they were forced to face. The work's still lucidity and immaculate timing invoke an almost spiritual transformation of the physical space. Initially a performance poet, SuAndi's works are a heightened form of writing, a form that enables her to combine linear narrative with the ability to concurrently expose successive layers of fact and symbol. By examining inter-racial relationships and experience, her work extends black tradition to embrace a wide range of black experience, challenging the propensity of black as well as white to confine black experience.

Vaishali Londhe
Eligibly Yours **(1994)**
Photo: Robert Taylor

Maya Chowdhry
The Sacred House **(1993)**
Photo: Ali Zaidi

70

Keep on running   Catherine Ugwu
The politics of black
British performance

The ability to speak of the complexities of the black British condition can also be seen in the work of artists Dorethea Smartt and Shirlee Mitchell and the younger artist Vaishali Londhe.

Dorethea Smartt, whose live art works originated in a desire to perform her poetry, and Shirlee Mitchell her collaborator, use slide images and voice simultaneously to invoke meaning, the impact of voice being intensified by overlaying a visual element. *Medusa* - a short text/slide piece performed by Dorethea, uses projected images of Medusa along with those of herself, friends and family to create parallel histories based on the similarity of their experiences and reality. Through these symbolic acts of recovery she initiates a dialogue which addresses the politicised aesthetics of identity. Using the metaphors of hair, mistaken identity and self respect, Smartt reclaims the myth of Medusa, herself and her community. This piece suggests that any radical analysis of British culture, and in particular the black female artist, must address this liberation of the self and the recovery of black cultural lineage.

Eligibly Yours, one of Vaishali Londhe's first performance pieces, addresses the difficulties of living within a society unable to comprehend the cultural practices and pressures of another. A tape/slide piece based on vox interviews, it is a response to pressures from her family to secure a marriage 'before it's too late'. This work compares and contrasts the methods and ideologies of western dating agencies and Asian marriage bureaux. Reflecting her exposure to both Asian and western cultural images, she deconstructs the methods of two cultures to 'secure the ultimate union'.

Londhe uses cardboard signs to reflect the power of language in determining our relationship to the past, present and future. Laying them out across the front of the performance area, she begins to place them around her neck, until she becomes so entangled in them she is unable to move. This act highlights the specific role of language as an instrument of power, emphasising how a series of fragmented, unconnected and conflicting words, can, over time, create myths which become part of dominant belief systems. It is an act of empowerment over language.

One concern central to the work of a number of black live artists is the strong desire to initiate complex and often contradictory dialogues, around some of the most contentious questions of our time. The work engages audiences across cultures and generations with questions often too daunting for us ever to imagine how we could begin discussion in any other forum. By layering meaning, live artists are able to frame several often contrasting concerns in tandem.

Maya Chowdhry's piece, *The Sacred House*, overwhelms the viewer with slide and video images, ranging from talking heads to complex visual metaphors, to explore issues of identity. Layered on top of this is a complex soundtrack, live text and actions performed by Chowdhry, dressed in a tartan sari.

She draws parallels between exclusion on the basis of ethnic origin and exclusion because of sexual preference. As a black woman and an artist, she demands the right to express what the identity of such an individual might be and provide an alternative to assumptions about race and sexuality. It is a proclamation of the inner life of a black gay woman and an implicit affirmation of the use of art as critical and symbolic gesture.

Such attempts to deal with several inhabited subject positions can be seen in the work of many black artists. Subodh Rathod, for example, whose controversial subversion of traditional South Asian dance forms addresses contemporary issues of sexuality, homophobia, race and racism, has proved to be contentious both cross- and inter-culturally.

> Black cultural workers must constitute and sustain discursive and institutional networks that deconstruct earlier modern black strategies for identity-formation, demystify power relations that incorporate class, patriarchal and homophobic biases, and construct more multi-variant and multi-dimensional responses that articulate the complexity and diversity of black practices in the modern and post-modern world. *Cornel West*[13]

Deployment of a diversity of media, often simultaneously, along with a bombardment of

Keep on running   Catherine Ugwu
The politics of black
British performance

Ronald Fraser-Munro
Quack FM **(1994)**
Photo: Robert Taylor

Sarbjit Samra
Hysterical Asians (1994)
Photo: Ray Jones/
Derek Kingston

Keep on running   Catherine Ugwu
The politics of black
British performance

disconnected and reconnected symbols, actions and images is indicative of live art practice. This method assaults the senses with loaded images, forcing the viewer to translate received objects, actions and words and construct meaning. Ronald Fraser-Munro's *Quack FM* is a perfect example of the disorder produced by being out of sync with, and having a complete disregard for, dominant media images. *Quack FM* is a performance representation of a strange audio/visual radio programme, beamed from a deep space colony of 'outcasts'. Throughout the piece, Fraser-Munro inhabits the characters of a bunch of extra terrestrial DJs, each more peculiar than the last - a ragamuffin, a klan member, a wayward monk, a sex kitten - all human possibilities in all their sickness. With the use of large scale slides, bizarre video projections and a hypnotic and relentless sound-track, he creates a weird self-contained world. Unregulated and unrestrained, it is representative of the absurdity of our condition.

His provocative use of stereotypes, humour and his abrasive diatribes against social, cultural and artistic rules continues to elicit both adulation and disgust amongst audiences. His publications/fanzines and use of the soap opera form in his recent piece *Il Mal Di Pal - Mutant Hero Trespassers,* are delightful and brilliant examples of avant garde critique bought home and adapted for mass consumption, integrity intact.

Sarbjit Samra's *Hysterical Asians* is a solo performance which explores how meaning is enforced, given value and becomes naturalised as 'real' simply through the process of repetition. *Hysterical Asians,* using 'rhythm' as a device, reflects the obsessive desire to consume fixed representations and questions how ideology secures its power through the seduction of entertainment and the banality of its repetition. Standing centre stage - a cultural and sexual transvestite - wearing garish traditional Asian dress, excessive make up and jewellery and a cowboy hat, holding an Oscar and microphone, Samra gushes with delight at being able to perform for us. A backing tape plays a crass country and western record, Samra lip-syncs and dances along, endlessly repeating the experience as the song ends, and then begins again.

> Let us remember that, whenever we encounter repetition in cultural forms, we are indeed not viewing 'the same thing' but

> its transformation, not just a formal ploy but often the willed
> grafting onto one culture of an essentially philosophical
> insight about the shape of time and history. *James A Snead*[14]

For some artists the location and siting of work is of paramount importance. Simply relocating live work from traditional art spaces into 'other sites' can subvert the nature of art itself, illicit an unorthodox encounter between artist and viewer. A number of artists have incorporated a live element within durational gallery-based installations. By exploring space and time they provide other ways of engaging and interpreting the work.

Chila and Magic Burman's installation - *Ice Cream and Magic* - is a site-specific gallery piece which fuses a range of media including video, music, live interaction, mural-painting, text and food preparation. It manipulates images of past and present to blur artform boundaries and supplicate alternative narratives, capable of reflecting the multiplicity of identities which make up the British Asian experience. Chila Burman's work over the years has used a wide range of forms, including printmaking, photography and video, to persist in her determination to reclaim authorship and obliterate subservient representations of Asian women.

The video-manipulated family photographs and home movies explore the experiences of Chila and Magic's parents who ran ice cream, magic and retail businesses in 1950s Liverpool. These images collide with clips from Hindi movies and film of Chila kung fu fighting. Unable to reconcile the images, the viewer is forced to experience the feelings of fragmentation and disorder common to marginalised groups. These sensations are heightened by the soundtrack, which mixes music from a range of cultural influences - 90s bhangra co-exists with ragga and rap. Both artists are present as art objects, Chila seducing each individual viewer with gifts of food and Halloween masks - encouraging and enticing them to interact.

Kumeljit Kaur Lillian's durational performance/installation - *The Master's Case* - subverts the ritual of shoe-shining to explore master/servant relationships. Simply by placing this powerful action in the unfamiliar context of a gallery space, the artist provokes a broad range of feelings in the viewer. Loaded with historical and cultural references, the work

76

Keep on running
The politics of black
British performance

Catherine Ugwu

questions the internal difficulties around serving and being served, caring and being cared for. An attempt to exorcise the horrors and humiliations of slavery and reassert mastery over a rich black cultural legacy, this is an act of empowerment for the future.

There are few contexts for artistic practice more hazardous and ambiguous, difficult and ambitious than those outside the accepted art circuit. Actions placed outside institutions in the public domain are likely to engage with unpredictable responses. The public in such arenas are inevitably more raw in their response, more candid and vigorous in their commentary than the 'well-trained' viewer.

Keith Khan's *Flying Costumes, Floating Tombs* - a large-scale, site-specific performance piece - is one example of this type of engagement. Staged in London and Bristol in 1991, the piece included 156 artists from a wide range of disciplines including dance, costume, carnival arts, music, and visual art. *Flying Costumes* explored the processes involved in cultural transference and ownership. Drawing its theatricality from carnival, the work depended on the centrality of the viewer. A collaboration of immense proportions, it embraced the creativity of many, never regulated or controlled by any one artist at the exclusion of others.

Keith Khan's remarkable contribution to this area of practice, both as an artist and activist, should not go unmentioned. Working in visual and costume art, performance, carnival and film, he consistently produces innovative, exciting and visually stunning pieces which challenge the aesthetic boundaries of a range of artforms. Blurring formalist distinctions, Khan emphasises hybridity, utilising the visual devices of set, light, fabric, colour, as well as the costumed and clothed body, to subvert notions of taste and originality.

Moti Roti, Puttli Chunni, created in collaboration with Ali Zaidi, typified this collision of artforms: 'film and theatre, popular drama and high art, Hindi/Urdu and English; film music and photography. It was unashamedly high spirited and brash. It was geared towards changing perceptions of Asian theatre and showing that work emerging from the community could be challenging.'[15]

Not only does segregation in our society occur on cultural, economic and social grounds but also spatially. Space is divided and shaped by the physical presence and symbolic force of buildings, monuments and landmarks. These architectural structures invariably represent one dominant interpretation of a particular historical event. Their ability to invoke, reinforce and sustain dominant interpretations of particular historical moments is immense. The impact on our lives of these structures should not be underestimated. They are the evidence of a past littered with inequity, inscribed onto the present, a painful legacy of power and its symbolic representation and effect. Architectural structures are reminders of the absence of parallel and other histories from the visual landscape.

Some live artists work to engage audiences in connecting architecture to lived reality, encouraging us to examine and analyse the symbolic force of buildings and urban spaces in our lives. They highlight the importance of landmarks to our sense of home and belonging. The work of Visual Stress, a loose collection of artists based in Liverpool, clearly engages with these issues. Most of their works are located in public sites and performed to large crowds who are encouraged to become active participants in the performance rituals.

Urban Vimbuza, a piece staged on St. George's Hall Plateau in Liverpool city centre, was a celebration of cultural diversity in the shadow of eminent monuments constructed to celebrate Britain's colonial conquests and its contribution to histories of enslavement and oppression. This piece clearly highlights how public sites and landmarks, if occupied, can undermine the memory and legacy of dominant histories and narratives, and reveal new and alternative stories and truths.

Utilising music, visuals, performance and pyrotechnics the piece deconstructed a range of local, national and international images, cultural monuments and icons. Actions, performed to incapacitate the symbolic political and economic power of the location and the cultural influence of its surrounding buildings included pyrotechnicians spitting fire 'in the faces of bronzed statues - icons of white male heroes of the city's industrial past and the nation's colonial glory... much prized was a statue of General Gordon whose

78

Keep on running   Catherine Ugwu
The politics of black
British performance

colonial conquest/barbarism in Sudan was depicted by him standing on the shield of a Sudanese warrior'.[16] One act of symbolic representation, replaced by another.

Public encounters of this kind attempt to offer cultural strategies which can meaningfully intervene in the present. Cultural activism is able to re-map the boundaries in issues of difference, nurture and transform public engagement within public space. Groups such as Visual Stress clearly attempt to enter this terrain, working from and with the local community. Merging activism with spectacle, the act of art making is clearly an act of empowerment.

Mobile Auto Mission, performed by Visual Stress a few days before Christmas in 1992, continued to address the power of public space and architecture to the maintenance of established histories. The work was a day-long public procession through Liverpool city centre in which a convoy of vehicles visited a series of twelve historically oppressive public sites. Stopping at each location, the performers enacted rituals to expose legacies of bigotry, denounce and exorcise the unchallenged and unwritten collusion of the spaces in the slave system.

Mobile Auto Mission was commissioned for *Trophies of Empire* - a large scale collaboration between visual and live artists, producers and venues that took place in the three ports of Bristol, Hull and Liverpool. Central to all events in *Trophies of Empire* was the importance of location and context. The message of the project was clear: that a discrepancy exists between the fictitious unity of identity Britain has claimed, and the multiplicity of identities it must now represent if it is to retain its legitimacy as the guardian of national identity. Fifteen artists were commissioned to produce work for the event, all of whom were asked to offer a personal response to the historical legacies of British colonial exploits and the histories which chart their rise, decline and impact.

Whilst researching the project, visual artist and curator Keith Piper explored the evidence of imperial legacies in the three participating cities: 'some are highly visible, others remain obscured and unexcavated. They permeate the very social, physical and economic fabric, manifesting themselves in ways varying from place names, public monuments and buildings, to the presence of whole communities of people.'[17] Here,

Piper identifies the narrative power of location, site and context and the possibilities it holds for artistic practice.

> The modern black Diaspora problematic of invisibility and namelessness can be understood as the condition of relative lack of black power to represent themselves to themselves and others as complex human beings, and thereby to contest the bombardment of negative, degrading stereotypes put forward by white supremacist ideologies. *Cornel West*[18]

Artists engaged in live art and related practices have received meagre support and precious little understanding or encouragement over the years. This has however, not prevented them from creating work that is exploratory, highly challenging and unrepentantly abrasive.

After so many years of exclusion, and so many battles to represent the diversity of black experience and determine meaning within our culture, the recognition of difference is now seen as a threat to dominant power structures and the way in which these structures interpret the world. As such, self-appointed guardians of culture have directly attempted to affect the existence and visibility of artistic practice by a plethora of strategies, actions and devices.

Efforts to curtail artistic freedom of expression have come from a range of interest groups and communities, from both within and outside the art world. All these attacks are a response to the politicisation of a growing number of contemporary artists working across artforms. These artists engender fear. Their work highlights what we try to hide, demanding that we look to ourselves, threatening established cultures and their supremacy, which has historically bestowed so much in return for so little. Attacks on artistic practice have gone beyond the airing of opinions of dislike, disagreement and outrage and moved into the realm of direct censorship.

This impulse is clearly evident in the US, less vibrant and more covert in the UK. Right wing politicians and representatives of the moral majority on both sides of the Atlantic

Keep on running
The politics of black
British performance

Catherine Ugwu

have denounced and castigated experimental work, condemning it as dangerous and menacing. This reaction is based in a fear of the consequences of artistic and cultural encounters which invite audiences to reflect on their contemporary condition and challenge the established norms and conventions which create and sustain it.

This backlash in the USA has resulted in direct attacks on the policies of the National Endowment of the Arts in an attempt to silence the voices it funds. Artists from marginal groups and areas which dare to attack formal notions of arts practice depend upon public subsidy to support the development of their work.

Political pressure on public funding organisations has a far-reaching impact, the ripple effects witnessed as a result of this right wing backlash are immense. Private sponsors become cautious, frightened by the repercussions of supporting anything which might spark controversy. Art institutions begin to shy away from presenting the most difficult and challenging work or attempt to modify and passify it prior to presentation, for fear of fighting a battle in the public domain. Those that do not, risk the withdrawal of both public and private financial support. Work which overtly embraces material of a political and sexual content is scrutinised by the media, policed by politicians, funders, art institutions and their curators.

More common, harder to detect and even more difficult to resist are the subtle actions which reduce the visibility of the work by limiting access to art institutions. Appropriation becomes more intelligent and ingenious.

The influence of black British theatre practice, fighting to be heard in the 70s and 80s, in raising some of these issues cannot be underestimated. Cuts in funding, apathy and the loss of many individuals and companies from the artistic arena throughout the 80s and early 90s has brought traditional black theatre practice to its knees. The recent and recurrent cries by critics, funders, artists and audiences, which proclaim the death of black theatre, have not looked to the margins for encouragement. What we see within current live art is black theatre reinventing itself, refusing to be contained and appropriated. By relocating resistance to different sites, artists effectively continue the battle against inequity in more complex and ambiguous terrains.

Criticism which dismisses work of an experimental and politicised nature as borderline, average, not good enough, or not art at all, suggests that the work is too influenced by social concerns, relinquishes formal artistic considerations to a principal concern with subject matter, and is harmfully over-identified with its audience. Such criticism rarely addresses the work directly and consistently neglects the institutional and historical context within which the work is shown. This attitude only highlights questions: whose values, whose quality, whose aesthetics?

To appreciate the impact of the work currently being produced by black live art practitioners in Britain, we must look for a new vocabulary which aims to contextualise and legitimate their achievement.

> Instead of an authoritative position, in which criticism reaches for the definitive judgement of value, it may be helpful to conceive of it as an ongoing conversation or dialogue that seeks to deepen our knowledge of the way texts 'work' as they circulate in the contingent and contradictory circumstances of the public sphere. In this approach, it is not even necessary to construct a general or definitive framework for interpretation, as what arises instead is a practice of interruption, which does not aim to have the last word on the aesthetic value of a given text, but which recognises the contextual character of the relations between authors, texts and audiences as they encounter each other in the worldly spaces of the public sphere. *Kobena Mercer*[19]

No longer misled by the belief that representation in the cultural arena will translate into equity, artists have developed numerous means of resistance and found a hundred ways to respond to and survive oppression and the actions which maintain it. Reappropriating, reinventing, trying to stay one step ahead, artists continue to move their work outside the 'official' art circuit and into public space, hoping that there it will avoid containment and restraint. Alienated artists come together and form alliances, creating communities of

82

Keep on running
The politics of black
British performance

Catherine Ugwu

resistance, communities of like-minded individuals.

All the work being created by artists engaged in live art or related practices, some of which I have discussed above, can be seen as a critique of the timidity and the unadventurousness of a large amount of the output of black performance and theatre in Britain in recent years. Using these actions, interventions and engagements to decry the complacency of black creativity, live art lays down the gauntlet to other black artists to invade the temples of high art, public institutions and the more ambiguous sites of ideological control. If all else fails, enter even if not invited, act rather than discuss, empower rather than plead.

With thanks to Andrea Phillips who edited this paper.

1   Cornel West, 'The New Cultural Politics of Difference' in *Out There: Marginalization and Contemporary Cultures*, ed. Russell Fergerson, Martha Gever, Trinh T Minh-ha and Cornel West (MIT Press & Museum of Contemporary Art, New York 1990)

2   Kobena Mercer, *Welcome to the Jungle: New Positions in Black Cultural Studies* (Routledge, London 1994)

3   Guy Brett in Art In America (November 1989)

4   Isaac Julien, 'Climbing the Racial Mountain: a conversation with Isaac Julien' in *Small Acts: Thoughts on the Politics of Black Cultures* by Paul Gilroy (Serpent's Tail, London 1993)

5   Ibid.

6   Guy Brett in *Mona Hatoum* (Arnolfini, Bristol 1993)

7   Ibid.

8   John Cage as quoted in the introduction to the catalogue of *Twenty-five Years of Performance Art in Australia* curated by Nick Waterlow (Ivan Dougherty Gallery, Sydney, 1994)

9   Rhodessa Jones, Theaterforum No.31

10 Ralph Ellison, *The Invisible Man* (Penguin, London 1989)

11 Coco Fusco, 'Passionate Irreverence: the Cultural Politics of Identity' in 1993 Whitney Biennial Exhibition Catalogue (Whitney Museum of American Art & Harry N Abrams Inc., New York 1993)

12 CLR James in *Welcome to the Jungle* by Kobena Mercer, op. cit.

13 Cornel West, op. cit.

14 James A Snead, 'Repetition As A Figure of Black Cultures' in *Out There: Marginalization and Contemporary Cultures*, op. cit.

15 Keith Khan, in publicity for his work *Moti Roti, Puttli Chunni* (London 1993)

16 Michael McMillan, report to the Arts Council on *Urban Vimbuza* by Visual Stress (Liverpool, 1988)

17 Keith Piper, introduction to *Trophies of Empire* catalogue (Bluecoat Gallery and Liverpool John Moores University School of Design and Visual Arts in collaboration with Arnolfini, Bristol and Hull Time Based Arts, 1994)

18 Cornel West, op. cit.

19 Kobena Mercer, op. cit.

RIDING THE TIME LINE
Nina Edge

Location

I am twisting the telecommunion between costumes and players, musicians and budget, organising fragments for forthcoming Liverpool Lives.

In October 1994 Liverpool Maritime Museum opens its Transatlantic Museum of Slavery (Against Human Dignity). To mark the occasion Visual Stress (MCs Keith Higgins and Jonathan Swain) will orchestrate rites of passage for the lost souls of capital exchange. A procession which unites New Orleans funerary blow-out with Afrocentric ablution will assemble to ride the time line. Nobody knows how many mourners will arrive, nobody knows how many souls will depart.

So I twist the telephone jug attempting the delivery of thirteen feet of skeleton - a costume made in collaboration with Cheshire Youth Theatre for Bones of the Earth last year. If the bones have not been buried, I will dance them dockside with Visual Stress, the assembled company and the dearly departed.

Visual Stress on Albert Dock will probably not be viewed as black performance art, although there will be black in it. Even the definition factory of high art cannot quite get a handle on the act and the result of collaboration between one black man, one white man and a cast of hundreds. Whilst it contains white, it is unlikely to be called black, unlikely to be contained in the 'marketable bracket of "black performance art" '.[1]

Meanwhile the capital exchange continues as Liverpool's cultural servicers brace themselves for the final onslaught in their campaign to win their bid as 'City of Architecture'. A request for a two minute bit of live arrives. I suggest that Cardiff

Nina Edge
Limpieza de Sangre
Ferens Gallery, Hull (1992)
Photo: Nina Edge

Nina Edge in *Zong*
A collaboration with
Visual Stress and Cheshire
Youth Theatre
Liverpool (1994)
Photo: Katherine Noonan

performer Paula Smith inhabits the guise of the Statue of Liberty, I inhabit the guise of Kali, and that we make live two female power icons. All creation & all destruction. All ancient and all modern. All liberty and all capture of the old new world, used as a background for the re-marketing of the new old world. Appropriate perhaps for the architects of festival handout culture.

The term 'art' has diverse meaning for diverse peoples. The presentation for the City of Architecture bid is unlikely to be described as art: it is an act of marketing. High power art is essentially a self-referential insider debate; a linear monologue.

My production as an artist has involved dialogue, one of my primary concerns being to communicate across language, culture, gender and age differences. The more sophisticated my production becomes in achieving these objectives, the more difficulty high art specialists experience in placing and evaluating it. Art dead or live, which does not collude with the linear monologue, is rendered partially inaccessible to western critical frames.

The canons of high art production reduce forms that fall outside its jurisdiction by either prefixing or trailing them. Top of the range we have *pro-celebrity art* (practice), then a sliding scale to *community access art* (projects) and *art kit* (hobby). Attachments to the art world range through Primitive, Naive, Folk, Women's, Black and Live; a pocketful of prefixes assigning reduced status. Visual artefacts emanating from outside the Western high tradition are attached to the country or culture of origin, particularly if the makers are black, and particularly if the origin is already documented and defined by Western anthropologists.

I am delivering planting instructions for a garden collaboratively designed with the young women of The Green Youth Connection and their neighbours in Cardiff's docks. Within a spate of development corporation offerings, the garden is regarded by many as the only installation that reflects the diversity of homelands of the docks' population. My capacity for diverse design, which includes the black heritages alongside the white, is expected of me. My working knowledge of the English (Welsh) garden is not. But lavender is a low maintenance plant.

Broad audiences defy the high, and present themselves as sophisticated and informed thinkers if they are able to get within viewing range. The spaces in which live art can take place can be the ordinary public spaces of the park, the street, the wasteland. The invisible limits which prevent entry into gallery spaces are dissolved. Live events can refresh the audiences that other forms ignore.

Corporate Masquerade
Live art is attractive since it seems to have a flexible definition, a short history and an open mind. I have very little experience of live art practice, but enough to know that it is formally mediated as something located in modern history.

Art history itself is an illustrated history of Western ideology which has effectively transmitted itself globally to the point where its principles now dominate. This history has no black participants, only black subjects. In the clean new space of live art this exclusion might be felt less because there is less history to be had around the category.

I am dressed in a black and white shirt. My colleague Mr Mike Stubbs is wearing the same. We are identically dressed and wearing conference badges reading *Prontowipe Bulk Erazer*. Standing amidst shredded paper, people, contracts and rubber stamps, we process a line of people, helping them fill out contracts, prontowiping in panoramic trays of salt and seeds. Discs, videotapes and cassettes are splattered all over a stylish black magnet beneath images of communication technology. This is the office, the bureau of *Prontowipe Bulk Erazer*, where uniformed workers are offering the service of

Prontawipe Bulk Erazer
**A collaboration
between Nina Edge
and Mike Stubbs (1991)**
Photo: Nina Edge

Art isn't only a 'provided' activity; people do it anyway.

This is not like peeping in the gallery comments book, this is not like reading the press. This is like a queue of shoppers sharing the same checkout, like going to the stadium as opposed to watching the coverage on television. There is no commentator decoding the action, naming the players or defining the rules. You are on your own, outriding the time line of Western art history.

PRONTAWIPE

Fed up with junk mail?
Too much paperwork?
Bombarded with information
extraneous to your needs?
Old photos causing distress?
Bills, demands, reminders irritating
you horribly?
Dog eared coupons, photos, leaflets
and lists lingering for too long?

Documents, photos, video, computer disks, memories and more disposed of
quickly and hygienically at our new PRONTAWIPE office.

**FOR YOUR FREE
INTRODUCTORY WIPE**

Visit our friendly staff Mike & Nina
at our new office in the foyer of
the Royal Festival Hall, London.

26th – 27th February.

Or send your material to us on:
Tel: 071 921 0847 Fax: 071 928 2049

ritual disposal of unwanted or worthless information. We are offering etch-a-sketch quickies, free advice on how to set up a home Prontowipe, shamanistic rituals and free erasable gifts to take away. Biscuits carrying hand-crafted icing slogans are nibbled by punters who turn to read the day's contracts, proudly displayed in the office. This is information disposal; this is information exchange. I am shredding a copy of E H Gombrich's *Story of Art*. It is an immensely enjoyable activity. For all involved.

The spectacle and illusion of *Prontowipe Bulk Erazer* was commissioned as part of a season of live art by Projects UK in Newcastle. It was the first collaboration between myself and Mike Stubbs, and has run three times to date. It was funded under an umbrella of live art, but departed from the normal manifestation of this form. The audience were so integral to the piece that it could not function without them. The artists who produced the work were born of homelands so diverse that you could see it in their skin. Multi-cultural if you like. Part of the audience were fooled by their surroundings, asking how head office could be contacted and a booking made to clean up the dirt elsewhere. Authentic illusion.

Officers at the Arts Council of England and regional arts boards, who operate 'combined arts' or 'live arts' departments, confirm the need for creative endeavours that refuse simple categorisation and artform separation. Perhaps an infrastructure based on artform definition lacks validity, since the definitions available don't expand to the breadth of contemporary cultural activities. The pre-defined limits of live practice in theatre or dance do not encompass all movement or all enactment. The combined and live might provide chinks in cultural edifices which allow a new mix of essences to emerge. Unfamiliar recipes including combinations and actions which cannot be easily named or placed. State funding of the combined and the live might provide a chink in the apparatus through which contemporary work of merit can receive support.

The culture of black makers might easily find footing in live art or combined art, since a heritage of symbiotic culture, of fusion and interconnection between forms, makes the work uneasily named or placed. I cannot identify if this apparently progressive space is also a siphon which pumps innovation away from other live arenas, or a one-way valve which draws black energy onto very small patches of land. Is it progress to trade one prefix for two?

The conceptual framework that combined departments provide, coupled with the events staged by city councils, development corporations and festivals, has recently delivered dynamic, challenging, and resonant experiences for a diverse audience. The scope of audience type, size and interest is vast, in the live arena, with large spectacle-based events taking place outdoors in town or country. The high can content itself with the tip of the iceberg whilst the live and the symbiotic processes and products of the black deal with the greater mass, which is submerged.

Art isn't only a 'provided' activity; people do it anyway, whatever their proximity to quango money, professionals or education.

My brother's granny-in-law is a Gloucestershire woman in her eighties. For most of her adult life she had designed and made costumes for young people in her family to wear on fancy dress parades. It was something she was very good at. Every year she won the contest. As she described her costumes, she catalogued major media events of her era, from the moon landing to punk. All of these had been re-embodied in her costumes, which were made as gifts of attention and skill to young family members. Symbiotic native British culture is a remnant of its former self, but nevertheless it remains, lodged in rural areas, and in generations who can remember their own power to make culture. Granny's snaps of the annual parade provide an expansive portrait of contemporary psyche and experience. Try looking for an equivalent in an exhibition catalogue. Women like her have been transmitters of creative power, like so many of all races and cultures who knit and stitch their way to freedom. They have encouraged and informed my practice, and, despite apparent difference, they will sit as soul sisters alongside the great women of carnival production. I will sit beneath them and look up. Have we escaped with the treasure?

Live art - public art
In June '93 I was interviewed as a prospective candidate for the post of Town Artist in a small British coastal resort. The presentation was a bit of a performance.

The panel sought a public artist to invigorate the image and economy of a seaside resort in decline. I had seen public art commissions on varying scales across the country. The emphasis of this sector on producing permanence was apparent. Sculptures installed in some UK cities threatened a permanence beyond the life of the buildings amongst which they resided, and perhaps a permanence beyond their useful life as ciphers of contemporary culture. Surely public art could be time-based.

At the interview I presented past work and attempted to convince the panel that the greatest public artwork of all is exciting because it is live. It is public in that it is made publicly; is of and by the public; it is an attraction because the gathering of peoples is of itself a spectacle; it is dynamic because it cannot be controlled, predicted or measured. It has value because it cannot be owned, traded, stored or commodified. It is an attraction because it happens on a time line of a day or two, and, if missed, will be re-incarnated through the telling of tall stories. It would resound in local history through oration, hence achieving location and permanence in memory. A permanence beyond the installation of a bronze or stone erection or indeed beyond the installation of any fixture.

It would be there forever, or for as long as its audience and makers had need of it; for as long as it was useful.

Like a day at the fair, like bonfire night, like seeing a goal in extra time - like a million events which enter collective memory and outlive the solidity of stone installations, roads or buildings. The importance of an event in the memory, an event in experience, or an event as described has minimal maintenance cost, and achieves maximum permanence through employing ephemeral means and collective energy.

Live art - public art - may be reconstructed through documentation, imaged through photography, video or film. It may be remembered and described. Nothing however, would reproduce the experience of being there, bearing witness and being witnessed on the day, at the time. This experience would be both personal and collective: audiences experience each other, audiences experience art.

The invisible has a potency beyond the visible, a life beyond the fickle inquisitors of fashion, taste and aesthetic dogma. The power of the invisible is a force to be reckoned with. To site a permanent structure as public artwork is to place a fact in the townscape. The staging of a live public art event is to induce a legend in the space known as living memory. Those in town on the day could be participants, player-participants, audience-participants, maker-participants, missed it, received it second-hand.

Just how public would you like your art ?

Long distance
I invoked heritage and tradition in support of the live case.

Aware of the relationship between the traditional and the contemporary in art production, I boldly asserted that such acts of culture were native British traditions interrupted by the needs of a state which demanded a centralised value system in order to undertake a large colonial task. The unification of belief in Britain, around Queen, church and country, dispensed with rolling cheeses, corn dollies, dancing straw men and burning wicker figures; vital pagan leftovers. The communal enactments of fertility, joy, fear, and mania were banished. Even the magical and protective assets of native plants were forgotten. Instead, the power class engaged in bio-twiddle, importing and hybridising species from the southern colonies. State education enabled the population to name the Seven Deadly Sins, obliterating the Seven Sacred Herbs of the druids.

Thus the symbiosis was thrown out with the bath water and a new centralised culture was constructed. The establishment of standard British time along the bony metal fingers of the railways united the nation under a time-based grip. The broad base of public production and the ownership of culture was whittled away in favour of a new professional class of educated artist, who usurped even the journeymen masons and sculptors of Romanesque and Gothic spires. The diverse regional cultures of the common wo(man) were obliterated, along with the common land, and replaced with the systematic hierarchies of 'applied' and 'fine' art. Eventually it had to happen: art schools were invented, endorsing notions of gentility and genius.

Culture had entered the enclosures, but nothing could hinder a small southwestern seaside resort from liberating it, I argued, in the tradition of the new Britain; the Britain in which Kittitians in Leeds, Islanders in London, Punjabis in Leicester, Pakistanis in Bradford had brought the fatted calf back home.

Perhaps I was a healer, a panel member suggested (thus implying sickness): if the act of collective transformation is invigorating, raising energies and banishing sluggishness from the cultural circulatory system then perhaps my work would have a healing aspect. I agreed, somewhat taken aback. However, the brief was aimed at economic and image regeneration. Would my potential appointment herald an era of seaside health-spa gatherings?

Not. Ask Bill. The Criminal Justice Bill.

Carnival, (or something close to it) - the ultimate public artwork, the live work evaluated and accessed in production and performance by young and old, genius and trader - was not the winner in this arena. At least not this time around.

Close up
Picture the scene;
A few moments have passed since the performance ended. The audience are released from their passive bondage as viewers. They stampede the bar; the noise is hearty.

There again;
A few moments have passed since the performance. The participants emerge, walking the wire between adrenaline rush and blood sugar drop. They are bracing themselves; they are exposed beyond the exposure of actors; they lack the protective shield provided by writers, directors and producers. They have autonomy, responsibility. They cannot easily pass the buck.

Logistics make the live art available in real as opposed to virtual terms. It is barely possible to avoid the scrutiny of the audience, since both are concurrently present. This is not like peeping in the gallery comments book, this is not like reading the press. This is like a queue of shoppers sharing the same checkout, like going to the stadium as opposed to watching the coverage on television. There is no commentator decoding the action, naming the players or defining the rules. You are on your own, outriding the time line of Western art history.

Audience meet eyeball to eyeball with the live artists. The energy that this dynamic produces is different from the interface between art object and audience. Since time-based events bring audiences together for viewing, they function as social as well as intellectual events. Although the same work can be seen on several occasions, in different venues, the experience cannot be repeated. The ambience of the audience forms a part of the event, particularly in the context of modern urban societies, where isolation is a fundamental social experience. When performers and audience enter the live arena - real time with synch sound - it is likely to be memorable merely for having happened at all, regardless of the merits of the work. The bravery of artists who are prepared to expose themselves in front of a live audience is memorable. Performers gamble on the success of their work with little or no market knowledge. Nobody knows who will be in the audience, what their agenda or response might be. In doing so they risk failure.

I am rushing across town to catch a student performance, bags banging, coat flapping, eyes down on the watch dial. I don't want to miss it. As I near the venue - a derelict near the city centre - steady streams of audience converge. Casual passers-by, driven by curiosity, join the flow. Here we go, all wondering what will happen. Then everyone sees the police car; we all know the event is over without it having begun. After pausing to enjoy the moment, the audience evaporates, the artists are thwarted. The performers risk damage to their reputations incurred by the omnipresent unreliability factor.

Calculate, for example, another risk: the female Asian population in the UK stand odds of 60:1 on being physically attacked whilst going about their business on the streets of Britain. Risk is relative.[2]

The proximity of live product to producer and viewer is alien to mainstream gallery practice, where intellectual barriers born of education; physical distance born of the touring show; or visual language barriers born of culture, preserve the void between maker and viewer. The illusion of genius is better maintained by the employment of 'the safe distance'. Audience can write in a comments book, or phone up and complain. A funder might withdraw the money supply, a work might be sold or praised, but on the whole, quietly. How safe is the distance? How long is a piece of string?

Audience performance

After the opening event, the art hangs alone.

In the gallery, the audience rarely speak, greet or establish eye contact. Gallery spaces are quiet arenas. A viewer magically steps aside, freeing the zone of the focal point on the approach of a stranger. One viewer steps out of the optimum viewing position, another steps in. A slow motion queue passes through, separated by invisible barriers. The barriers are complex in Britain; they are the combined force-fields of age, race, class, gender, region - any signifier of identity.

When I first began to examine how my work impacted on its audience, the works I made were not live, but installations in various media, presented in art and non-art spaces. My methodology was to hang the work, attend the opening event, re-enter the space unannounced at a later date and then to eavesdrop with intent. This system only worked if I removed images of myself from the space, and if I masqueraded as a casual passer-by, disguised as audience. Informally and invisibly performing.

I am loitering in The Bridge Gallery at the (then) Polytechnic of Wales, pursuing a policy of exhibiting in both black-identified and mainstream arenas, resisting the duality of the ghetto walls that act as both protective buffer and restrictive enclosure.

It is the anniversary of Armistice Day, November 1990. I am curious about audience response to a series of new ceramic and batik works. The work includes four war memorials, which remember specifically black British, black European, black African and black Asian contributions and losses.

Already permanently installed in the gallery is a wooden relief that remembers local white Welsh losses. It is decorated with freshly gathered paper poppies. This solo exhibition, *Out of My Tree*, also remembers so-called accidents like Bhopal; Soweto; and the appropriation of the Swastika. From Tantric to Teutonic.

I am loitering with intent.

The audience are using two focal lengths, leaning and peering at the small, stepping back to read the large. They have assumed the body language of pecking birds. I hear them say the things which strangers say when they are presented with objects which make them think about that which might otherwise be carefully avoided. Some people can't remember what happened at Bhopal; they ask for an artist's statement, for clarification. They have never seen a batik depicting a fried egg before; they have never heard that Bengal food producers starved after feeding the allies in Europe. Some people think the artist must be bitter, others think the artist must be sweet. I am kissed by strangers and overseas students who are familiar with the wall. I am described as a protest artist in the local press. Another wall to trap an artist whose world view might extend beyond that of the mainstream.

Even a blind fly on the wall would know that some of the pecking birds were black, whilst others were white. In this way I discovered the relationship of identity to memory, value and aesthetics. I witnessed a gulf between the mainstream and marginal audience, and discovered patchy common ground.

The tools I used for the static acts of communication are those exploited in contemporary mass audience visual culture. Beauty, humour, description, saturated colour. Stock tools of the trade. I also used ancient technologies such as batik or ceramics, consistent with those associated with a producer from the 'third world'. Some of my visual means were clearly of Asian descent. I noticed how this was considered appropriate: the more authentic the better. My batiks, however, were seen favourably for knowing their place, being of Asia, of the ancient and therefore unlikely to stand as equal contender with the modern, the Western, the real and fine Art. Curious, particularly since I have been upbraided by white textile experts for not producing genuine traditional batik. (Whose tradition?)

Ethnic Cleansing is an ordinary installation, made of authentic British domestic and industrial supplies. Mop heads, J-cloths, nappies, shoes, a genuine British bomb, a traditional English plastic table cover and a couple of best sellers. The spiritual essence of this piece is the same as any batik I have made, yet it has been regarded as confusing: not representing myself and my people quite properly with reference to my perceived heritage, despite the fact that I have as great a cultural umbilical to the UK as to any other territory. Curious: the batiks are made with genuine British dye.

Entry

I entered live life through requests to perform or make, as part of another artist's live practice. My role has been defined as a visual technician asked to carry out a particular task, within a particular length of time. The tasks always produced a physical visual outcome. The various results could always be seen during the performance (spice drawing, for example, in *Chavil Ki Chadder* with Keith Khan & Co.). I could be invisible, building structures or, later, items worn, carried or used by performers (in *Flying Costumes, Floating Tombs* with Keith Khan & Co.). I could be both visible and invisible, providing large images, costumes and props made before the event, and making paper and batik during the event (in *Verbal Images* with Levi Tafari & Co.).

The works I entered as visual technician were black productions. They involved many people; were social, spiritual and cultural gatherings. A spell in a black production is invigorating and informative, providing a spiritual buoyancy when tides in the mainstream threaten death by drowning. I left these events inspired, informed with new skills and new notes about audiences.

There was no looking back. I made and performed as a puppet in *Giant Kali* for the Puppet Centre Trust in London, played Kali again for *Forest Voices* (with Deborah Jones & Co. in Cwmcam). These events returned black forms into white arenas. I co-founded and designed and played for the Tiger's Costume Club in Cardiff (with the Trottman/Griffith family) returning black form to black people in Diaspora. Great gatherings.

In the live arena expert types might consider how to assign correct titles to events, begging the question: what is my title, where did it come from and am I at liberty to be myself, despite skidding between standard definitions?

Page 98
Keith Kahn
Flying Costumes,
Floating Tombs **(1991)**
Photo: Ali Zaidi

Page 99
Nina Edge
Kali **(1993)**
Photo: Paul Roberts

I have lived for twelve years in Cardiff, enjoying the luxury of the old and mixed dock communities. The descendants of over forty homelands have bubbled away in Butetown for generations. These peoples are extremely sophisticated in their mediation of otherness, mixedness, blackness, Welshness and happiness. Would it were the same elsewhere.

Are you ticking as appropriate?		
Artist		☐
AKA	ceramicist	☐
AKA	textile worker	☐
AKA	sculptor	☐
AKA	writer	☐
AKA	performer	☐
AKA	carnival designer	☐
AKA	puppet maker	☐
AKA	theatre designer	☐
AKA	garden designer	☐
AKA	community collaborator	☐
AKA	educator/skill sharer	☐

Are you ticking as appropriate?		
Asian		☐
AKA	British Asian	☐
AKA	South Asian	☐
AKA	mixed	☐
AKA	non-white	☐
AKA	anglicised	☐
AKA	second generation	☐
AKA	third area	☐
AKA	country girl	☐

Absolutely yes. Next question.

The live audience arrive and depart together; they anticipate and consume together, they dwell in one space and time together. This lends the practice junior glamour, baby to the grown-up glamour of entertainers. The buzz factor is at large - there is potential for barriers to be smashed open or at least peered over. The fluidity of barriers, and apparent lack of preconditions, has lead me to plan further adventures in the live world.

Looks alive
The live art domain appears to be an un-charted territory. The regulating criteria of its practice are flimsy, disputed, difficult even to identify. This might liberate audiences and

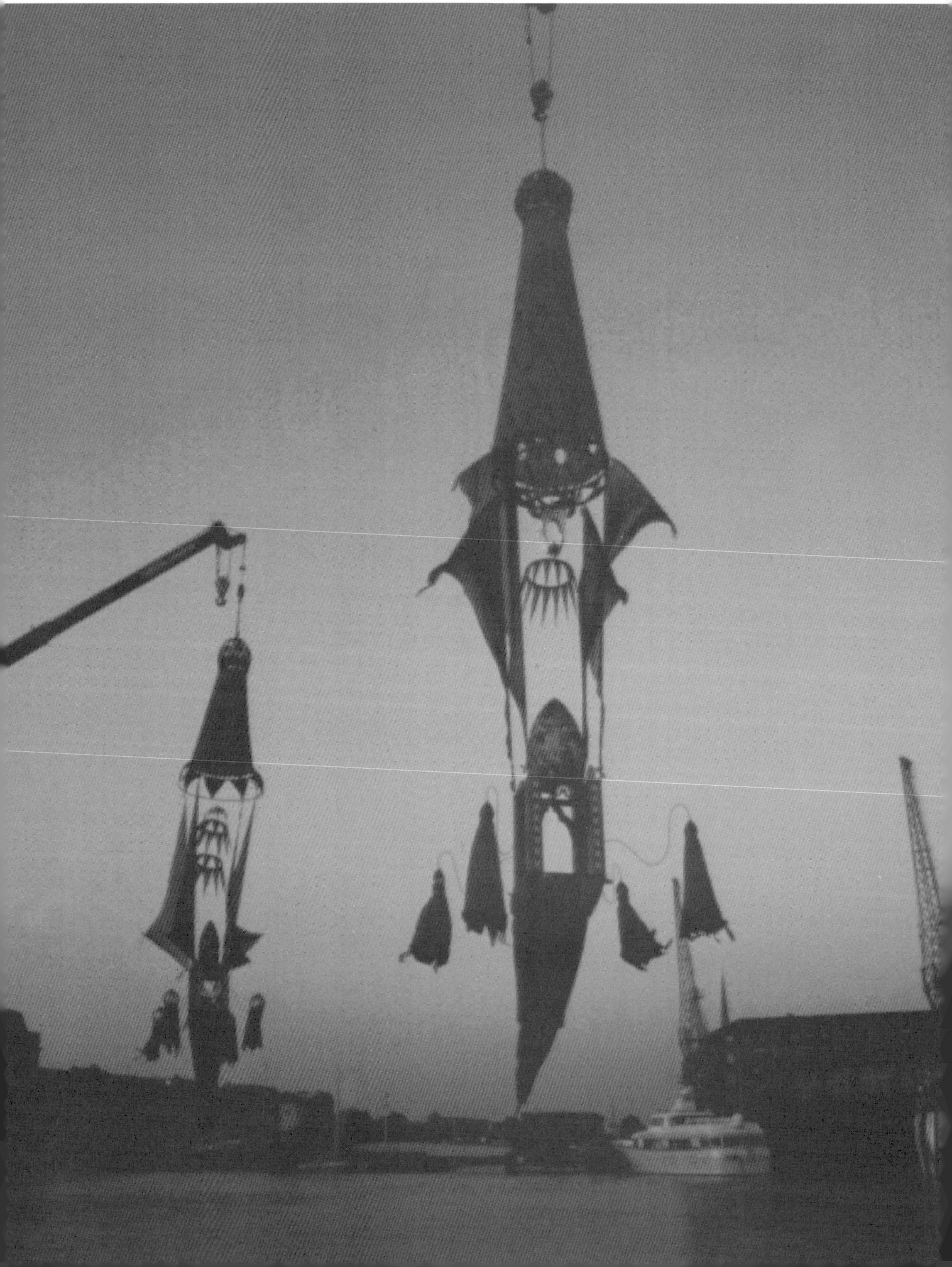

producers, providing a space where anything could happen. And that should mean anything for any person.

Formal storage and dissemination systems have failed to capture or document the essence of performance practice or the performance product. The critical analysis surrounding it is vague and appears speculative. I have no evidence for the systems upon which critical evaluation is based. This looks a lot like freedom. The space provided by forms which do not drag tomes of historical signposting in tow, such as live art, or media art, hold a particular attraction to those artists whose identity already has them in the vicinity of the margins. Forms which have only recently been named are almost like new countries, ripe for all who wish to stick their flag into the topsoil.

But the new land is in many ways the same as the old land, since it is populated by the same people, who have not laid down their baggage before entry.

Black practitioners are watched obsessively, with the close-up attention of heat-seeking infra-red. They are watched for danger and they are watched for hope. As of course it should be, since black, and particularly African people in Diaspora, in providing for themselves, also provide the ex-colonisers with a power house of contemporary creative excellence, rivalled by none, emulated by all.

As if addicted to catharsis, a sector of audience clearly has as a hobby coping with the controversial; a formalised vulnerability. Being prepared to be shocked, beyond shocking, ready for anything, forms an aura of superiority around senior punters. Medals of liberal cultural achievement can be collected on the live art scene, which has the reputation of raising the tired spectres of controversy and transgression. Attendance provides opportunity to demonstrate empathy, experience, education, tolerance and confidence around a margin. However, if the performance doesn't deliver the anticipated punch, then there might be trouble anyway.

Looks familiar
On the occasions of performing as visual technician in *Verbal Images* (with Levi Tafari & Co. in 1992, commissioned by the Bluecoat Gallery and Hull Time Based Arts, and

performed in Hull, Liverpool and Scunthorpe), I noticed audiences held assumptions about what the prefixes 'live' and 'black' would deliver out as culture: what they might expect for their money. Whatever they were expecting they did not (all) get.

Furthermore, my role as visual technician - performing tasks to another artist's brief - did not exist in the external frame of reference. The journey (wo)man, or artist in symbiosis, may be ordinary in black production. She is, however, extraordinary in the mainstream. However black it was, it evidently wasn't the particular black sought by its audience. How appropriate was it to show the work as part of the Root Festival of Live Art in Hull? Audiences found the work too skill-based to get an art title. Not black enough, not live enough, not fine enough; art entirely lacking reference to mainstream live art practice, but maintaining reference to all sorts of other things.

Some clearly know what they want from the novelty packs of black, live, art. If it fails to meet expectations, news from the edge craved by the centre is devalued on the basis that it does not fit mainstream subject indexes, or look authentically of distant homelands. Roll out the mehendhi, bring me my Yellow Bird and let us all feel Hot Hot Hot, just don't call it art.

Indulging current taste has always been a means of survival.

Who will taste benevolent surveillance; checking the mythologised black male, seeking Asian mysticism. Who will taste multi- and cultural-looking events, the appeasement of guilt, the denial of pain, the hearty good humour? Who will find me a passive Asian woman?

I am standing on the precipice of Virtual Duality surrounded by white powders and security grilles. This time the townspeople have entrusted me with over three thousand keys. In return I am preparing an invitation. Come with me, exchange words with the Word Doctors and their attending Vision Doctors. Lets make a spectacle of ourselves. The time is now, but how, when and who has been sold down the river?

The spirits of the betrayed burn on Merseyside Dock in 1995 in a live art work entitled *Sold Down the River*, in collaboration with the Bluecoat Gallery, as a result of a proposal conceived and written during my year as Henry Moore Sculpture Fellow at Liverpool John Moores University. I shall be launching burning figures and raising a spectacle of enactments appropriate to the theme. The invitation to participate is open to all comers, as is the event. The time is now and this time the description will read Nina Edge & Co.

Collect your energy.

1   Live Art Magazine, London, September 1994
2   Home Office data, 1991

Dan Kwong

Susan Lewis

SuAndi

Reza Abdoh

Elia Arce
Reza Abdoh

Chila Kumari Burman
Elia Arce

Chila Kumari Burman

Ronald Fraser-Munro

Guillermo Gómez-Peña
Ronald Fraser-Munro

Reza Abdoh

Kif Higgins

Elia Arce

Chila Kumari Burman

Kif Higgins

Rhodessa Jones
Ronald Fraser-Munro

Guillermo Gómez-Peña
Rhodessa Jones

Dan Kwong

Dan Kwong

Kif Higgins

Susan Lewis
Susan Lewis

Guillermo Gómez-Peña

SuAndi

Rhodessa Jones

Reza Abdoh

SuAndi

Elia Arce

Dan Kwong

Chila Kumari Burman

Susan Lewis

Ronald Fraser-Munro

SuAndi

Guillermo Gómez-Peña

Kif Higgins

ARTISTS' PAGES

Rhodessa Jones

Reza Abdoh is a New York-based theatre-maker, writer, director and film-maker.

Co-founder in 1991 of the performance company Dar A Luz, his live works have toured to theatres and festivals throughout Europe and America.

Incorporating text, music, film, movement and costume, his performance work challenges received notions across a range of contemporary issues including sexual and cultural identity, life, death and the modern urban experience.

Recent live works include:
Quotations From a Ruined City (1994), *Tight, White, Right* (1993), *The Law of Remains* (1992 USA, 1993 Europe), *Simone Bocanegra* by Verdi for Long Beach Opera, California (1992), *Bogeyman* (1991), *The Hip Hop Waltz of Eurydice* (1990 USA, 1991 Canada, 1992 Europe).

Video and film works include:
The Tryst (1993), *The Blind Owl* (1992), *Daddy's Girl* (1991) and *The Weeping Song* (1991).

Photos by Paula Court, courtesy of Dar A Luz

REZA ABDOH

Tight White Right

Coon, Coon

Black Baboon

Brutal, Worthless

Thieving Goon

Often High ... Thrives in Jail

His Welfare Cheque

Is in the Mail

Tony You wanna be on TV Blaster? **Tom P** Yeah
Tony And what's your tale? **Tom P** I got on the bus yesterday
and there was a white lady sittin' on the bus and she had some
sweet smellin' perfume on and a black lady got on the bus and sit
down behind her said 'Oh honey what in the world is that sweet
smellin' perfume I smell?' Little white lady looked up and said,
'Black Night black bitch a hundred dollars an ounce' Oh this made
the little black lady mad The black lady let out one of them corn
bread cottin pickin' farts *Fart sound* the white lady said, 'Oh my God
what is that terrible smell I smell?' The black lady said, 'White beans,
white bitch, fifteen cents a pound'.

Tony Look at me I'm aching inside; longing to know who your enemy is Blaster. We'll make you an idol. We'll televise your death, your birth, your power, your fire, your desire, your rage. We'll teach you to twist turn blow rant rave and we'll teach you to walk through the valley and we'll teach you to scream, eat shit and bark at the moon. Blaster I'm aching I'm aching I'm longing to know who your enemy is. Look at me Blaster, look at me. Can't you win for losing?
Tom P I can't win for losing, and if it wasn't for bad luck I wouldn't have any luck at all. But things are bound to get better 'cause they can't get no worse. I'm just like the blind man standing by a broken window *Crash* I don't feel no pain. It's your world.

I am Iron Man

Leader of the Ku Klux Klan

Wearing sheets so white

Killing Niggers in the night

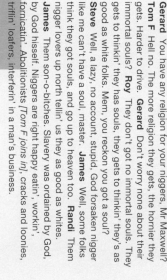

Gerard You have any religion for your niggers, Mr Maxwell? **Tom F** Hell no. The more religion they gets, the hornier they gets. Harder to drive. **Gerard** Don't worry none about their immortal souls? **Roy** They don't got no immortal souls. They gets to thinkin' they has souls, they gets to thinkin' they's as good as white folks. Mem, you reckon you got a soul? **Steve** Well, a lazy, no account, stupid, God forsaken nigger like me can't have a soul, master. **James** Well, some folks think they got souls, and go up to heaven too. **Randi** Them nigger lovers up north tellin' us they as good as whites. **James** Them son-o-bitches. Slavery was ordained by God, by God hisself. Niggers are right happy eatin', workin', fornicatin'. Abolitionists [*Tom F joins in*], cracks and loonies, triflin' loaters, interferin' in a man's business.

Tony	Blaster, pack your bags you're leaving.
Tom P	Where am I going?
Tony	Home.
Tom P	This is home.
Tom F	This isn't home nigger.
Anita	Dead boy in the dusty street.
Randi	Who will be the witness?
Dana	I will be the witness.

REZA ABDOH

Elia Arce is a performance artist,
writer, director and film-maker.

Born in Costa Rica, she has been living in the United States for
twelve years. She has worked with
the Bread and Puppet Theater and
co-directed and performed with the
Los Angeles Poverty Department
(LAPD) for five years.

Recent live works include:
El Otro Lado/The Other Side, for
the Festival Latino in LA and
Jupiter 35 with LAPD. Her first
full-length solo performance work,
*I Have So Many Stitches That
Sometimes I Dream That I'm Sick*,
premiered at Highways, LA and
was presented at ICA, London.

In 1993, Arce received a J Paul Getty
Foundation Individual Artist
Fellowship and in 1994 a Rockefeller
Multi-Arts Production Grant which
facilitated the production and
touring of *Stretching My Skin Until
It Rips Whole*, her latest solo
performance work.

She is co-founder of the
Interdisciplinary Institute of Art and
Technology in Costa Rica, the first
institute of its kind in Central America,
which will open in 1996.

ELIA ARCE

Your think is your space. I think is your space. We agree, we get along fine, we agree. You have to teach me how to live in your space so I get to stay. I don't want you to teach me anything. Teach me how to rob you. Teach me how to rob you. We get along fine, we agree. Do we still agree? Teach me how to live in your space. I want you to teach me everything. You want to leave about me. So you can have less than what you had before and I can have more than what I had before, and get even. I rather be here being part of the stealing than over there being stolen from. Do we still agree? ... until I take it from you and make it mine until I take it from you and make it mine. Your space that was mine and not mine until I take it from you and make it mine. I make my space by stealing some of yours. I make my space in here. I need room to make my space in here. I am here in your space. I was born here but this is your space. But me is mine only. Leave me alone. I need room to make my space in here. I leave about me. So you can have less than what you had before and I can have more than what I had before. I was born here. I am here. We are here.

ELIA ARCE

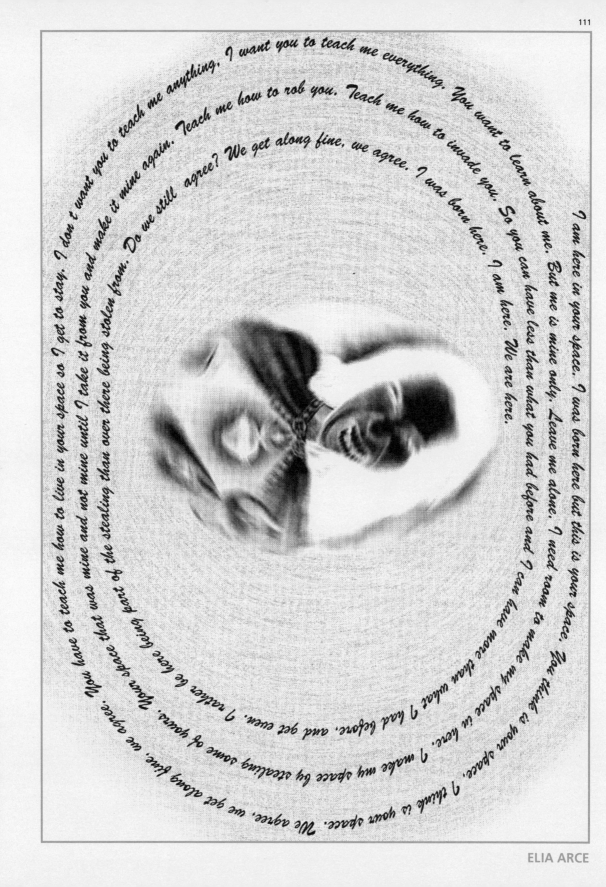

I am here in your space. I was born here but this is your space. Your space is your space. I think is your space. We agree, we get along fine, we agree. You have to teach me how to live in your space so I get to stay. I don't want you to teach me anything, I want you to teach me everything. You want to learn about me. But me is mine only. Leave me alone. I need room to make my space by stealing some of yours. Your space that was mine and not mine until I take it from you and make it mine again. Teach me how to rob you. Teach me how to invade you. So you can have less than what you had before and I can have more than what I had before, and yet even. I matter be here being part of the stealing than over there being stolen from. Do we still agree? We get along fine, we agree. I was born here. I am here. We are here.

Chila Kumari Burman is a visual and installation artist, photographer, film maker, writer and performer. Born in Liverpool, she is currently based in London.

Her work has been exhibited in the UK, Europe, Canada, Cuba and America. A persistent theme in all her work is her determination to reclaim authorship of representations of South Asian women by obliterating dominant and enduring stereotypes and images.

Recent group exhibitions include: *Uncommon Thread*, Civic Theatre, Johannesburg (1995), *Portrait of My Mother*, International Signals Festival of Women's Photographers, French Institute, London, Edinburgh and Paris (1994), *Femme Noir 21st Century*, Manchester and London (1994). *May 5th HAVANA Biennale*, Cuba (1994), *Recontres au Noir*, International Photo Festival, Arles, France and Washington DC, USA.

Recent solo exhibitions include: One person show, Watermans Art Centre, London (1995). *Fax Art Poster Project*, Pavilion Leeds (1994) and *Body Weapons*, Stockholm, Sweden (1993).

Recent videos include: *Ice Cream and Magic I and II* (1994) and *Body Weapons and Wild Women* (1993). Her most recent live work (produced in collaboration with Magic Burman) *Ice Cream and Magic* (1994) was staged in Manchester, London and Copenhagen. A monograph on the work of Chila Kumari Burman has recently been published by the Institute of International Visual Artists (inIVA).

Page 214: Photo from Ice Cream & Magic, ICA, London 1994, by Robert Taylor

CHILA KUMARI BURMAN

CHILA KUMARI BURMAN

AUTOMATIC RAP

CHILA KUMARI BURMAN

DON'T GET ME STARTED. GIDA PA.

SO MUCH TO SAY, TO SAY, THIS IS THE HARDEST THING IN THE WORLD, FIRE, FIRE, FIRE, AGG, AGG, AGG,

ONE STRUGGLE AFTER ANOTHER, ONE FIGHT AFTER ANOTHER,

FREEDOM WHAT'S THAT? WOZ, IZ, DEAD HARD, STEREOTYPES REINFORCE MYSTERY

NO ART BOOKS ON OUR SHELVES AT HOME. NO PAPER TO DRAW ON. JUST MAKING ICE CREAM 99S

TIGER NUTS & TOFFEE APPLES AND MILLIONS OF TOFFEE WALKING STICKS - ART SISTER ART

NO ONE LISTENS, SUPPOSE THEY MUST ALL THINK IT'S DEAD EASY, THEY HAVEN'T A CLUE.

MAKING ROTIS NIGHT AFTER NIGHT, NO TIME FOR HOMEWORK, BUT LOADSA SWEETS TO EAT FROM THE ICE CREAM VAN, CORNETTOS,

CHOC-ICES & RASPBERRY SPLITS. FLAKES AND SCREWBALLS, SHELLS AND BOATS...

WHO SAYS ALL WORKING CLASS ASIAN GIRLS ARE QUIET, WHA' IN OUR HOUSE? WILD GIRLS, PUNJABI, BHANGRA,

GIDHA, STICKY SWEETS, SWEAT, WHO'S WEARING THE BEST SALWAR KEEMICH, GLITTERY, SATIN, & VELVET RAGE,

GIDA PA, GIDHA PA GORIA, DANCE ENGLISH SISTER DANCE. MOVE THAT BODY...

ROTI, DAL & BEANZ & BISCUITS, PARMA VIOLETS, HOPSCOTCH UNDER THE DIM COBBLED STREET LAMP IN BARE

FEET IN FRILLY NYLON FROCKS, TATTY HAIR, RED CORDUROY DRESSES, SPARKLY JURIDAR PYJAMA, WHITE, PURPLE & PINK INDIAN FILMS

EVERY SUNDAY AFTERNOON, ALL DRESSED UP, TEARS, NAPPIES, PLAYING IS IN THE AISLES,

CHOCOLATE, COKE, JALEBI, LUDU, BARFI, AND SYRUPY SWEET WHITE MASALA TEA, BAR 6, TOFFEE CRISP, GRAR

PAKEEZA, MOTHER INDIA, PHOOLAN DEVI, JHANSI KI RANI, MEENA KUMARI, SITA DURGA MA, KALI, WHERE ARE YOU STANDING UP TALL &

REACHING HEIGHTS, SHOW'EM WHATCHA GOT...REBEL WITHOUT A PAUSE...

PROUD BRAND NEW GRAMMAR SCHOOL UNIFORM, WRONG HAT, 11 PLUS, CYCLING PROFICIENCY, SWIM FOR THE SCHOOL

SHOT PUT FOR THE SCHOOL, FIRST CLASS HONOURS, WHO SAYS WE'RE ALL MEEK AND MILD SHARP AS A KNIFE...

FRAGILE EXPLOSIVE AND SENSITIVE SOULS HANDLE WITH EXTRA CARE AND LOVE.

WISH I COULD GO TO DISCOS, PARTIES, DANCES AND HAVE GIRL FRIENDS AND BOY FRIENDS LIKE ALL THE ENGLISH GIRLS AND POSH

ASIAN GIRLS, ANYWAY THEY'RE ALL LAST THOSE FELLAS, WIMPS, COULDN'T HANDLE US ANYWAY

WE'RE TOO WILD, SHARP, SMART, FAST, LOUD, DYNAMIC, SOFT SEXY AND SENSITIVE.

STAY IN, STUDY HARD, STUDY ART, BUY A STEREO FROM THE CATALOGUE, IT HURTS SO GOOD,

HIBERNATE TO LIBERATE - DON'T GET ME STARTED... LETS LAUGH AND DANCE

WORK HARD IN HABITAT ON SATURDAYS, ROB ALL THE BEST STUFF, FOR FREEDOM'S SAKE, WHY WORK?

STUDY HARD, TWICE AS HARD, HARD, HARD, HARD, MADNESS, SLAM, SLAM, SLAM, WORK, WORK, CARRYING A HEAVY LOAD,

STRUGGLE, FIGHT, SHOUT, IZZAT? RESPECT US NOW!

GOTTA MEK IT THROUGH THE NIGHT, WARM LOVE, SWEET PILLOW, YOU KNOW WHAT AM SAYIN DON'T CHEAT US

THE WORLD IS SO COLD, AIN'T DO NOTHING FOR YOUR SOUL.

COCKROACHES IN THE FIREPLACE, LOVE MASHING THEM UP, STIR IT UP LITTLE DARLIN', STIR IT UP...

THERE MUST BE HUNDREDS OF US DYING TO DO ART AND SING AND SHOUT OUT THERE,

WHY DID THEY HAVE TO MAKE IT SO HARD, GO FOR THE BURN, STRETCH AND TURN

BAD YOUNG SISTER, REACH OUT AND TOUCH, LET'S MAKE THIS WORLD A BETTER PLACE, WE SHALL OVERCOME

AIN'T NO STOPPIN US NOW, YOU NOW, HER NOW, WE'RE ON THE MOVE AND GROOVIN, CHULOR, LETS GO...

STRENGTHEN AND UPLIFT THE MIND... LETS GO CRAZY...

ROTI, KAPAR, AUR MAKAAN - FOOD, CLOTHING AND SHELTER. PEACE

CHILA KUMARI BURMAN

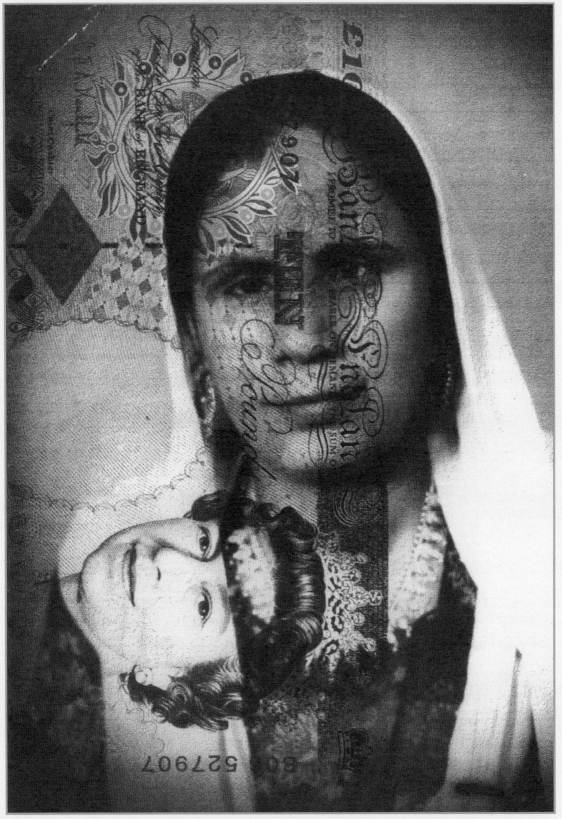

CHILA KUMARI BURMAN

Ronald Fraser-Munro is a writer, performer and media artist. Born in Cheshire and currently based in London, his interdisciplinary performance works have recently been staged in venues throughout the UK.

He uses humour, costume, text and video to subvert dominant stereotypes and media images of black people.

Recent live works include: *Le Chaise Longue Dangereuse* and *Bruder C'est Grim* (1994-5 - Barclays New Stage Award), *Quack FM* (1994 - A Black Arts Alliance Commission), *Il Mal Di Pal - Mutant Hero Trespassers* (1994), *Hey Up, Oswald* (1993 - An ICA Live Arts Commission) and *Old Blue Eyes is Black* (1992).

He is co-founder of and contributor to the publication le shovelle diplomatique.

Photos: Robert Taylor. With thanks to Black Arts Alliance

RONALD FRASER-MUNRO

Introduction:

My hatred of academia and institutions is well documented and I hope that my refusal to use any other but plain english (with an option on the esperanto) will cause extreme discomfort to all lovers of non-communicative language.

The name is Ronald Fraser-Munro. The height is brown. The language socialism cross bred with a malevolence gained whilst living in a world run by crelks. A crelk is an evil, hideous and bigoted creature in Cheshire folklore. That was the surface tension and now the head-numbing spirit.

It is my current understanding that somewhere in all my ideas and creations there are dark corners where my concerns lurk. I cannot imagine that I can suppress all these concerns, indeed I do not wish to because the continued abuse of the majority by the minority means that I am in the queue, on the list and had best be pro-active before I am in the ground. Naturally, the way I feel about the world I reside in informs my creativity.

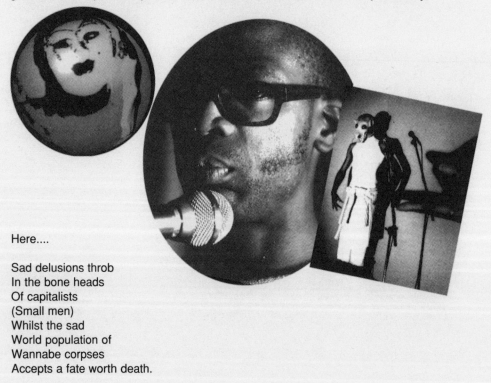

Here....

Sad delusions throb
In the bone heads
Of capitalists
(Small men)
Whilst the sad
World population of
Wannabe corpses
Accepts a fate worth death.

It might be believed (in comfortable minds) that suppression of creativity and free expression is very rare and applied only when necessary. This is typical of those lacking in imagination, emotion and street credibility. It is my experience that a wealth of humans deliberately attempt to mis-guide us (i.e. take us away from ourselves) either through ignorance, malice or a blend of the two. This seems foolish to entertain.

RONALD FRASER-MUNRO

No Waves, We're Friesian

Each artistic field
Has a clique of cows
Who eat but class
And then leave dung
In the educational
Background
All that bull
All that cow.

Where were we? Oh yes! Now it is all very well to encourage creativity and expression (in the hope it will lead to that ever illusive progression) but part of what I as see as the "creative brick wall" is the flock of promoters, performance practitioners and artists that seem interested only in those members of society who are the "art consuming" public. This may seem a little strong but the marketing of any gig indicates who is expected to attend. Add to this the cost of the ticket and what is being staged and a good percentage of a 100% congregation is lost to the devil for another night.

It is quite obvious that the Royal Opera House (a public venue, I believe) would be less enthusiastic about black patrons than say a Blues (a private event) would be about welcoming say John Major and his cabinet. I am sure either would be a memorable evening.

At this point I would like to make this statement:

I believe in "natural" artists (i.e. those who create from an inner desire or passion in opposition to those who chose art as a career following their institutionalisation). This natural creativity is in us all. Latent in some but there all the same. It is an energy, a force and therefore will out. I was tempted to say "Der Schnake" (daddy-long legs) then but I am advised against it and so instead......

That a generation of young people are not encouraged to experience theatre, performance, music, art and literature because it is never marketed towards them is a crime (although a merciful release in some cases).

Live Art has a unique opportunity in that it can be used to voice progressive ideas and break nasty old traditions and ignorance. If Live Art is to survive then it must actively engage youth, minorities, the old, the young, the dead, and by god the living. And yes, use a little seduction to realise that vision of progression so easy to forget.

Do you understand? Good!

overview of practice. an eagle's eye view

I have been at it for a long time
I played Charles Laughton playing Quasimodo as a child
I mimicked as a child.
I sang songs, daydreamed
Liked the darkness.
I wrote "poems"
And pulled strange faces.
Often my own.
We all did.
We still do
We always will.

A black male questions
Himself and his world.
And is told to stop
Crying over spilt blood
And to get on
With the hatred and anger
Like everyone else.
He obliges and is arrested
For gatecrashing a
Pyjamas and Barbecue party
In the typically Deep South....
And flamethrowing
The Christians partygoers.
There is little cheek, left, to turn.

RONALD FRASER-MUNRO

futile attempts to obstruct creativity.

Quite simply humans have the capacity to exist, make their time on earth mean something to themselves or to let others insert a (no doubt unwashed) hand up them and make with the glove puppet. "Lie to anyone you like but yourself", wrote Abbey Crunch the poetess in 1937. No other can stop our spirits and it is this which freaks the imperialists and fascists out.

history of practice. l'histoire de vomir

If society, and mankind at large, believes that civilization, democracy and capitalism has brought us to this golden age then these three grim reapers lead me to suspect, heavily, that we are all in very deep fly food. In order to describe my stance I first credit society and its followers with immaculate health and efficiency and for myself humbly accept "the sickness". I will never be well enough to take up my place in society and society will never be sick enough for me.

future of practice. morgen und morgen und morgen.

As I near the end of my comment I would hope that we are all at least of the accord that progress needs be best rubbed up (though not in the style of the seventies) in readiness for the next generation. As the alte weiss und noire batards (that fester parasitic upon the backs of the forgotten) prepare to suck our blood and souls dry we should be passing on some richness, some unsaleable gift, a spiritual loving kindness, a determination and strength, creativity and adaptability. We must pass it on. It cannot be kept if we are to continue. It was passed on to us.

Take care.

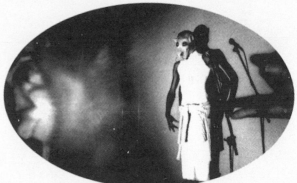

ROLE OF THE ARTIST:

I believe the artist has a responsibility to express (through creativity) those beliefs, emotions and feelings that may give an insight into the human condition. Encouragement is paramount to expression and communication and the artist is fortunate in having tools with which to communicate a message or idea. It is important that the artist communicates and is able to share ideas and work produced. Art is useless locked away in institutional vaults. Creativity and expression are not exclusive freedoms of the artist. If this world is to change (and it needs to radically) then we need every free mind and positive energy we can unite.

RONALD FRASER-MUNRO

Guillermo Gómez-Peña is an
interdisciplinary artist and writer.
Born and raised in Mexico City,
he has been resident in the US
since 1978 and is currently based
in Los Angeles.

Exploring cross-cultural issues with the use of performance,
multilingual poetry, journalism, video,
radio and installation art, his work
has been instrumental in the
development of debates on cultural
diversity, identity and US-Mexico
relations. His performance and
installation work has been seen in
theatres, galleries and at festivals
throughout Europe, America, Mexico,
Puerto Rico, Australia, Canada and
the former Soviet Union.

Recent live works include: *Mexarcane
International, The Year of the White
Bear, Undiscovered Amerindians Visit...*
and *Norte:Sur* (all collaborations with
Coco Fusco), *The Temple of Confessions*
(a collaboration with Roberto Sifuentes),
The New World (B)order and *Border Brujo*.

He is a regular contributor to the
national radio news magazine Latino USA,
he writes extensively for newspapers and
magazines in the US and Mexico and is a
contributing editor to High Performance
magazine and The Drama Review.

Photos: page 126 courtesy of Coco Fusco, page 128 by Neph Navas

GUILLERMO GOMEZ-PENA

The news from Aztlan Liberado

Good evening choliza, robo-raza and white minorities. This week-end has been a particularly intense chapter in the history of young Aztlan Liberado: Thirty-five Mexicanos have been executed by Anglo gang members. In an act of random violence, two unemployed corporate executives walked into a luxurious Taco Bell bistro and fired upon the peaceful fajita-eating customers. Today's headline in minority paper *The New York Times* reads, 'Blood and guacamole all over the walls; a macabre scene.' The police have surrounded residential East LA to block the entrance of angry gringo mobs protesting poor salaries and police brutality. The governors of Chihuahua and Sonora have issued a formal complaint to Waspanos on the West Bank who venture illegally into Mexican territory bringing with them dirt, diseases, drugs, prostitution and automatic weapons.

Anglo-mercenaries, ex-members of the defunct US army, in cahoots with various skinhead tribes, continue to attack several Chicano cities in the Southwest.

The political wing of the Anglo Liberation Front, the ex-Republican Party, finally went underground. Sub-commandante Buchanan has demanded amnesty for all political prisoners, the total restoration of the supremacist Anglo TV programming and the immediate reopening of all Protestant temples.

Buchanan's communiqué is in response to the up-coming Pacoima Trial, also known as the 'Raza Tribunal', which will begin next week. One hundred and seventeen gringo war criminals will be processed by a select jury of two thousand homeboys and ex-migrant workers. The defence attorneys are protesting the lack of Anglo representation in the jury. The most sinister war criminals include Pito Wilson and Darryl Gates, alias 'El Puertas', who are accused of rounding up over ten thousand Mexicans and confining them in concentration camps euphemistically called 'Juvenile Halls' and 'INS Detention Centres'. Gates and Wilson are currently being extradited by the Argentine government. Archbishop Matias has declared all Catholic churches sanctuaries for Waspbacks in defiance of the panic politics of Califas governor Molina.

Last week Molina issued an order to begin deporting 'insubordinate gringos who don't carry the national identity card'. She stated at a press conference held at Hotel Fiesta Aztlan, 'All Mexamericans must stick together in these transitional and chaotic times, and make sure that the illegal tax-evading Waspbacks do not continue to drain our economy and take advantage of our medical, educational, social and cultural institutions'. She clarified, 'This is not reverse racism, but mere financial pragmatism.'

I must say she's got a point. After all, thirty million vatos can't be wrong. For ABC Television Nacional Bilingue, this is Bob Sifuentes, fumigating your post-Colonial dreams.

GUILLERMO GOMEZ-PENA

GUILLERMO GOMEZ-PENA

The Cruci-fiction Project

On the evening of April 10th 1994, one week after Easter Sunday, Guillermo Gómez-Peña (dressed as a mariachi / bandito) and collaborator Roberto Sifuentes (dressed as a lowrider/gang member) crucified themselves on Rodeo Beach in the Marin Headlands Park, across the Golden Gate Bridge from San Francisco. This public ritual of 'spiritual transformation' was organised by Chicano curator Rene Yanez. The artists circulated the following statement amongst their audience during the performance:

If crucifixion was still an acceptable means to publicly ridicule and punish the heretics and 'public enemies' of the state, who would Governor Pete Wilson crucify? We are all gathered here at this peaceful beach to participate in a cross-cultural ritual for the end of the century. Unfortunately, ritual for a world in turmoil such as ours cannot possibility be devoid of political meaning. In the current anti-Mexican climate, politicians and mainstream media are blaming migrant workers ('illegal aliens') and Latino youths ('gang members') for the ills of our society. The politicians are holding up these cultural images as symbols of the decay of 'American values', the failing economy, social disintegration and the current crisis of national identity. In the Bible, small-time thieves Dimas and Gestas were perceived as public enemies and were left to starve to death on crosses next to Jesus Christ. Nowadays a similar punishment is being imposed on Mexicans ad Chicanos with the objective of further disenfranchising these communities. 'Tough solutions' (a euphemism for unilateral and authoritarian behaviour) to the 'problem' (whose problem?) of immigration and crime are being carried out before our very eyes; our access to medical and educational institutions is being restricted; Latino youths are being held responsible for urban crime and, despite the fact that Mexican immigrants are an essential part of the US economy, they are persecuted for 'stealing our jobs' and 'shrinking our budgets.' This is but a smoke screen to disguise the government's responsibilities. In other words, these vulnerable communities are in fact being symbolically crucified by the state. We have decided to expropriate the powerful symbol of the crucifixion and turn it around. We hope to transform an image of public ridicule into one of mourning, martyrdom, transcendence and empowerment. We encourage you to free us from our pain, and take us down from these crosses at the end of the event. Christ is missing today.

Guillermo Gómez Peña
Roberto Sifuentes

130

Kif Higgins is a multi-media artist,
musician and cultural activist based
in Liverpool.

His work with Visual Stress and
Rhythmic Stress has been seen
throughout Britain and across
mainland Europe. He regularly leads
and teaches performance art and
music workshops and has contributed
to number of conferences in Britain
including ArtBlackLive, Manchester
and LITTORAL, Salford. Working from
and with the local community, he
addresses the relationship of art and
the artist to a community and the
act of art-making as an act of
empowerment.

Recent live works with Visual Stress include: *Urban Vimbuza, Death by
Free Enterprise, Call to Arms/Cultural
Warfare, Mobile Auto Mission* and
Zong, Death by Free Enterprise part 4.
He is currently working on *Zong,
Death By Free Enterprise part 5.*

Recent works with Rhythmic Stress
include a sound system tour of
Switzerland, Holland, Italy and Spain
and a sound system and audio visual
performance for the opening event of
the Edinburgh Film and Video Festival.

He is currently working on a Rhythmic
Stress sound system collaboration with
artist Jamie Reid for an audio visual
installation performance.

With thanks to Peter Hagerty

KIF HIGGINS

| EXHIBITION TITLE | BLACK VARIATIONS | OBJECTS ARCHIVES | 7 |

| SECTION TITLE | CULTURAL DIVERSITY AMONGST NON -WHITES | SECTION NUMBER | 23. |

ACCESSION NO :   000.7273.w.o.w.

OBJECT/ARCHIVE DESCRIPTION : <u>BLACK LIVE ARTIST</u>

PRESENT LOCATION : <u>MARGINS OF WHITE ART WORLD</u>

DISPLAY POTENTIAL : <u>W.A.W. RESTRICTIONS APPLY</u>

WEIGHT / HEIGHT : <u>150 POUNDS / 6.FOOT 2 INCHS</u>

CONSERVATION REQUIREMENTS : <u>ETHNIC GRANT-AID</u>

ORIGINAL/ CLONED COPY : <u>1st GENERATION U.K.B.</u>

EXHIBITION DESIGN BRIEF

THE ARTS MUSEUM OF ENGLAND

EXISTING OR NEW NEG NUMBER

0030.094

TICK AS REQUIRED

AMOUNT REQUIRED ☐

OPEN DISPLAY ☐

CASE REQUIRED ☐

SPECIAL SECURITY ☐

REQUIRES PHOTOGRAPHING ☐

PHOTOGRAPH/ PHOTOCOPY OF OBJECT

Comments;   BLACK PERFORMER WEARING COLLAR
OF NON-WHITE ARTIST

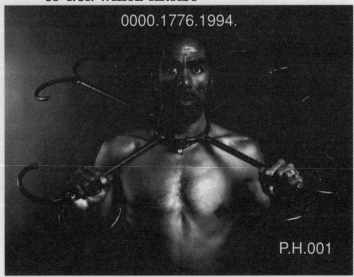

0000.1776.1994.

P.H.001

| EXHIBITION TITLE | BLACK VARIATIONS | OBJECTS ARCHIVES | 7 |

| SECTION TITLE | CULTURAL DIVERSITY AMONGST NON-WHITES | SECTION NUMBER | 23. |

ACCESSION NO.: 000.7549.w.o.w.

OBJECT/ARCHIVE DESCRIPTION : BLACK LIVE ARTIST

PRESENT LOCATION : MARGINS OF WHITE ART WORLD

DISPLAY POTENTIAL : W.A.W RESTRICTIONS APPLY

WEIGHT / HEIGHT : 150 POUNDS / 6 FOOT 2 INCHS

CONSERVATION REQUIREMENTS ; ETHNIC GRANT-AID

ORIGINAL/ CLONED COPY : 1st GENERATION U.K.B.

EXHIBITION DESIGN BRIEF

THE **ARTS MUSEUM** OF ENGLAND

TICK AS REQUIRED

AMOUNT REQUIRED ☐

OPEN DISPLAY ☐

CASE REQUIRED ☐

SPECIAL SECURITY ☐

REQUIRES PHOTOGRAPHING ☐

EXISTING OR NEW NEG NUMBER

0031.994

PHOTOGRAPH PHOTOCOPY OF OBJECT

Comments; BLACK SUBJECT PRACTICING WHITE ART TECHNIQUE   APPLICANT MODELLING FOR GRANT COMMITTEE

0000.1966.1994.

P.H.007

0000.1666.1994.

P.H.003

KIF HIGGINS

...istory and practice
...nius, the sexism and
...ork and cultural practice
... that attributed to a

...ant garde has multiple
..., "the avant garde
...gins." To be avant
...ribute to the
...t garde means to be
...rt between art and
...industrial,
...s of violence towards
...world countries. To
...in both artistic
...the world, not

...he avant avant garde
...formance art, then
...previously
...al practice.
...riting on
...the black community in
...together with those
...7)

...apart from there being
...ited, there were few
...Britain, or, since the
...hibition itself should
...is the tendency with
...But that british born
...practice and work
...individual experiences
..., sexuality, generation
...to the experience and
...ration of black artists.

...the dominant discourse
...performance art and
...performing
...instiutions, the

...ER · PEACE & FREEDO...

...WTON

FOR CONGRESS

KIF HIGGINS

G SOON,TO A CITY NEAR YOU
ACK PANTHER
ACE
NEWTON · S
CONGRESS
STA
BLACK PANTHER PARTY OFFICE, OAKLAND, CALIFORNIA,

KIF HIGGINS

Rhodessa Jones is a performer, writer, lecturer, teacher and political activist living in San Francisco.

She is Co-Artistic Director with Idris Ackamoor of Cultural Odyssey, a San Francisco-based multidisciplinary performance company whose solo and duet pieces have toured nationally and internationally. She is the Founder and Artistic Director of The Medea Project, a programme which promotes incarcerated women's self-awareness and self-esteem through the creation and production of theatre pieces based on personal histories. All her work is autobiographical and focuses on the use and power of art as a healing tool.

Live works with Cultural Odyssey include: *The Blue Stories: Black Erotica about Letting Go* (1992) and *Raining Down Stars* (1992), a collaboration with playwright Ed Bullins, jazz percussionist Don Moye and musician/performer Idris Ackamoor.

Other works include *The Mother of Three Sons* (1990 - staging and choreography by Bill T Jones), *Perfect Courage* (1991 - a collaboration with Bill T Jones and Idris Ackamoor) and *Big Butt Girls, Hard Headed Women* (1991).

Medea Project Productions include: *A Taste of Somewhere Else: A Place at the Table* (1994), *Food Taboos in the Land of the Dead* (1993) and *Reality is Just Outside the Window* (1992).

RHODESSA JONES

RHODESSA JONES

Coming of age in the eighties as a solo performer I felt it necessary, politically and socially, to develop a body of autobiographical work.

When I began dancing nude for money I called my grandma. I said, "Grandma Flossie, I'm dancing buck naked for money." My grandmother asked, "How much money?" I told her that if I worked real hard I could make a hundred dollars a night. My grandmother replied incredulously, "Yeah? Well you be the best buck naked dancer there is. You got to remember, there has always been show people in our family."

"The Legend of Lily Overstreet" - ©1979

My work is about transformation: mythical, spiritual, visual and physical. The power of communication as a social and political tool is vital in theatre: theatre that speaks to and for us all.

Big Mama said, "I won't live to see it, but before this thing is over, blood will run down the streets like water; there will be a plague upon the land; nations will be against nations; fathers against sons; mothers against daughters; and man will become a lover of himself - before this thing is over!"

"The Blue Stories: Black Erotical About Letting Go" - ©1992

I've always been a political activist. I've been blessed with the challenge of making art/performance with the disenfranchised, the incarcerated and the angry young. *What is art? Why do we make art? Who is art for?*

*The water is rising . . . heavy air
The chains, metallic taste in her mouth
    screaming, straining
Glistening in vomit, I am ashamed
Where is this place?
Bones are scattered everywhere.*

"Perfect Courage" - ©1992

*There is a man needing a quarter
There is a woman who lost her daughter
The stinkin' sidewalk screams with pain
Yes, it looks like rain.
And still we want to live here
Still we struggle and try
Still we want to live here
To live here and not die.*

"Food Taboos In the Land of the Dead" - ©1993
THE MEDEA PROJECT: Theatre for Incarcerated Women

I can not speak of my art without speaking of my life. Theatre saved my life.

> *That's my head, fallin' through the ceiling*
> *That's my soul you see*
> *Shining and reeling*
> *Come to buy pieces of a dream*
>
> "I Think It's Gonna Work Out Fine — A Rock & Roll Fable" - ©1989

In 1986 I was hired to teach "aerobics" at the city jail in San Francisco. Something else was called for.

> *Take it to the Ancestors.*
> *Build spirit catchers.*
> *This is a spirit catcher for one*
> *Regina Brown, age 27.*
> *   Regina: Daughter, Sister, Lover, Mama!*
> *Regina Brown, murdered in the*
> *Winter of 1989, after her second*
> *Release from jail.*
> *   Regina: Daughter, Sister, Lover, Mama!*
> *Regina Brown, mother of two children,*
> *Left here howling on the ground. A boy*
> *And a girl, left to make it in this hard luck*
> *Place called the world.*
> *   Regina: Daughter, Sister, Lover, Mama!*
> *Regina Brown, another whore with a heart of gold.*
> *   Regina: Daughter, Sister, Lover, Mama!*
> *Regina Brown, who, with a little direction,*
> *Could have been running the world,*
> *Or at least the World Bank.*
> *   Regina: Daughter, Sister, Lover, Mama!*
> *Regina Brown, one of my best drama students.*
>
> "Big Butt Girls, Hard-Headed Women" - ©1991

Politics don't work. Religion is a bit too eclectic, but art just might save us all.

Rhodessa Jones is a San Francisco performance artist, co-director of Cultural Odyssey, and founder and artistic director of THE MEDEA PROJECT, who can be contacted through her company, Cultural Odyssey, at 762 Fulton Street, Suite 306, San Francisco, California 94102, (415) 292-1850, FAX (415) 346-9163.

Ceramic sculpture: *The Storyteller* by Lorraine Capparell, 69 x 48 x 30 cm, 1994.

Dan Kwong is a Los Angeles-based performance artist whose work
combines autobiographical material,
social commentary and humour to
illuminate issues of social conditioning.

His work focuses primarily on the
re-definition of identity. His multimedia
performance works weave together visual
imagery, physicality and monologues to
offer a fresh insight into the Asian-
American experience. Having toured in the
US since 1990, Kwong made his
international debut in London with *The Dodo
Vaccine*, an installation and performance
presentation staged as part of *Extreme
Unction*, an exhibition of four Asian-
American artists responding to HIV/AIDS
(Panchayat, April 1994).

He is founder and curator of *Treasure In
The House*, LA's first Asian Pacific
American performance and visual art
series at Highways Performance Space.
He serves on the Board of Directors for the
18th Street Arts Complex in Los Angeles.

*Special thanks for additional photographs from Robert Taylor, Curtis Bean, Kathie de Nobriga
and Laverne Zabielski. Quotes from Lance Carlson, Judith Spiegel and Carmelo Rago.*

DAN KWONG

DAN KWONG

WENT TO SOUTH CAROLINA ~

— BROTHER TOLD ME I WAS "WHITE".

WENT TO SHANGHAI ~

~ 朋友 SAID I WAS "A.B.C."

Unction

Slowly, the alienation and hatred turned into self-hatred. The process by which external oppression is incorporated into the psyche, so that the victim becomes the perpetrator of his own persecution,

where, exactly, is home?

HIV
Aids
Ethnicity
Race

all the wild hopefulness

WRITE SHEET (REMOVABLE)

struggled to reconcile his tripartite cultural identities.

ROCK SALT

masculine grace

personal text is own experience.

internment of Japanese Americans

a refreshingly forthright approach to his often dark material.

DAN KWONG

Susan Lewis is a London-based performance artist. Her solo work has been performed throughout Britain and in the US. Recent live works include: *Walking Tall* and *Ladies Falling*.

She has choreographed for theatre companies including Black Mime Theatre Ensemble and regularly leads and teaches movement-based and performance art workshops. She has contributed to conferences in Britain and mainland Europe as a speaker and performer.

Winner of a Time Out/Dance Umbrella Award in 1993, Lewis has also been awarded commissions by ICA, London, Arnolfini, Bristol and shinkansen, London. Born in Britain of Vincentian and English parents, her social and autobiographical work explores the relationship between choreographed movement, performance, costume, sound and film. She seeks to channel a dynamic interaction of spiritual, emotional and physical energies into her working practice.

Photos: Ali Zaidi

SUSAN LEWIS

ladies

sugar, sugar, bags of sugar, still, ready made bags, sugar, sugar, bags of sugar,
sugar, sugar, bags of sugar, still, ready made bags, sugar, sugar, bags of sugar, still, ready made bags,
sugar, sugar, bags of sugar, still, ready made bags,
sugar, sugar, bags of sugar, still, ready made bags, sugar,
sugar, bags of sugar, still, ready made bags, sugar, sugar, bags of sugar,
still, ready made bags, sugar, sugar, bags of sugar, still, ready made bags, sugar,
sugar, bags of sugar, still, ready made bags, sugar, sugar,
bags of sugar, still, ready made bags, sugar, sugar, bags of sugar, still, ready made bags,
sugar, sugar, bags of sugar, still, ready made bags, sugar, sugar, bags of sugar, still, ready made bags,
sugar, sugar, bags of sugar, still, ready made bags, sugar, sugar, bags of sugar,
still, ready made bags, sugar, sugar, bags of sugar, still, ready made bags,
sugar, sugar, bags of sugar, still, ready made bags, sugar, sugar, bags of sugar, still,
ready made bags, sugar, sugar, bags of sugar, still, ready made bags,
sugar, sugar, bags of sugar, still, ready made bags, sugar, sugar, bags of sugar, still,
ready made bags, sugar, sugar, bags of sugar, still, ready made bags,
sugar, sugar, bags of sugar, still, ready made bags, sugar,
sugar, bags of sugar, still, ready made bags, sugar, sugar, bags of sugar, still, ready made bags,
sugar, sugar, bags of sugar, still, ready made bags, sugar, sugar,
bags of sugar, still, ready made bags, sugar, sugar, bags of sugar, still,
ready made bags, sugar, sugar, bags of sugar, still,
sugar, bags of sugar, still, ready made bags, sugar, sugar, bags of sugar, still, ready made bags,
sugar, sugar, bags of sugar, still, ready made bags, sugar, sugar, bags of sugar, still,
ready made bags, sugar, sugar, bags of sugar, still, ready made bags,
sugar, sugar, bags of sugar, still, ready made bags, sugar, sugar, bags of sugar, still,
ready made bags, sugar,

sugar, sugar, bags of sugar,
sugar, sugar, bags of sugar, still, ready made bags,

sugar,
sugar, bags of sugar,
still, ready made bags, sugar,
sugar,
bags of sugar, still, ready made bags,
sugar, sugar, bags of sugar, still, ready made bags, negroes, negroes, here
still, ready made bags,
sugar, sugar, bags of sugar, still,
ready made bags,
sugar, sugar, bags of sugar, still,
ready made bags,
sugar,
sugar, bags of sugar, still, ready made bags,
sugar, sugar,
bags of sugar, still,

sugar, bags of sugar, still, ready made bags
sugar, sugar, bags of sugar, still, ready made bags, sugar, sugar, bags of sugar, still,
ready made bags, sugar, sugar, bags of sugar, still, ready made bags,
sugar, sugar, bags of sugar, still, ready made bags, sugar, sugar, bags of sugar, still,
sugar, sugar, bags of sugar, still,
ready made bags, sugar, sugar, bags of sugar,
still, ready made bags, sugar, sugar, bags of sugar,
still, ready made bags,
sugar, sugar, bags of sugar, still, ready made bags, sugar, sugar,
bags of sugar, still, ready made bags, sugar, sugar, bags of sugar, still, ready made bags,
sugar, sugar, bags of sugar, still, ready made bags, sugar, sugar,
bags of sugar, still, ready made bags, sugar, sugar, bags of sugar, still, ready made bags,
sugar, sugar, bags of sugar, still, ready made bags,
sugar, sugar, bags of sugar, still, ready made bags, sugar, sugar, bags of sugar, still,
ready made bags, sugar, sugar, bags of sugar, still, ready made bags,
sugar, sugar, bags of sugar, still, ready made bags, sugar, sugar, bags of sugar, still,
ready made bags, sugar, sugar, bags of sugar, still, ready made bags,
sugar, sugar, bags of sugar, still, ready made bags, sugar, sugar, bags of sugar, still, ready made bags, sugar,
sugar, bags of sugar, still, ready made bags,
sugar, sugar, bags of sugar, still, ready made bags, sugar, sugar, bags of sugar, still, ready made bags, sugar,
bags of sugar, still, ready made bags,
sugar, sugar, bags of sugar, still, ready made bags, sugar, sugar, bags of sugar, still,
bags of sugar, still, ready made bags,
sugar, sugar, bags of sugar, still, ready made bags, sugar, sugar, bags of sugar, still, ready made bags,
sugar, sugar, bags of sugar, still, ready made bags, sugar, sugar, bags of sugar, still, ready made bags,
still, ready made bags,
sugar, sugar, bags of sugar, still, ready made bags, sugar,
sugar, sugar, bags of sugar, still, ready made bags, sugar,
sugar, bags of sugar, still, ready made bags, sugar, sugar, bags of sugar,
still, ready made bags, bags of sugar, negroes, negroes, here yet to be made,
the negroes came here ready made.
sugar, sugar, bags of sugar, still, ready made bags, sugar, sugar, bags of sugar, still, ready made bags,
sugar, sugar, bags of sugar, still, ready made bags, bags of sugar, negroes, negroes, here yet to be made,
the negroes came here ready made.
sugar, sugar, bags of sugar, still, ready made bags,
sugar, bags of sugar, still, ready made bags, sugar, sugar, bags of sugar, still, ready made bags,
sugar, sugar, bags of sugar, still, ready made bags, sugar, sugar, bags of sugar, still, ready made bags, sugar, sugar, bags of sugar,
sugar, sugar, bags of sugar, still, ready made bags, sugar, sugar, bags of sugar,
still, ready made bags, sugar, sugar, bags of sugar, still, ready made bags,
bags of sugar, negroes, negroes, here yet to be made,
the negroes came here ready made.
sugar, sugar, bags of sugar, still, ready made bags, sugar, sugar, bags of sugar, still, ready made bags,
sugar, sugar, bags of sugar, still, ready made bags,

SUSAN LEWIS

falling

sugar, sugar, bags of sugar, still, ready made bags, sugar, sugar, bags of sugar,
sugar, sugar, bags of sugar, still, ready made bags, sugar, sugar, bags of sugar, still, ready made bags,
sugar, sugar, bags of sugar, still, ready made bags,
sugar, sugar, bags of sugar, still, ready made bags, sugar,
sugar, bags of sugar, still, ready made bags, sugar, sugar, bags of sugar,
still, ready made bags, sugar, sugar, bags of sugar, still, ready made bags, sugar,
sugar, bags of sugar, still, ready made bags, sugar, sugar,
bags of sugar, still, ready made bags, sugar, sugar, bags of sugar, still, ready made bags,
sugar, sugar, bags of sugar, still, ready made bags, sugar, sugar, bags of sugar, still, ready made bags,
sugar, sugar, bags of sugar, still, ready made bags, sugar, sugar, bags of sugar,
still, ready made bags, sugar, sugar, bags of sugar, still, ready made bags,
sugar, sugar, bags of sugar, still, ready made bags, sugar, sugar, bags of sugar, still,
ready made bags, sugar, sugar, bags of sugar, still, ready made bags,
sugar, sugar, bags of sugar, still, ready made bags, sugar, sugar, bags of sugar, still,
ready made bags, sugar, sugar, bags of sugar, still, ready made bags,
sugar, sugar, bags of sugar, still, ready made bags, sugar,
sugar, bags of sugar, still, ready made bags, sugar, sugar, bags of sugar, still, ready made bags
sugar, sugar, bags of sugar, still, ready made bags, sugar, sugar,
bags of sugar, still, ready made bags, sugar, sugar, bags of sugar, still,
ready made bags, sugar, sugar, bags of sugar, still,
ready made bags, sugar,
sugar, bags of sugar, still, ready made bags, sugar, sugar,bags of sugar, still, ready made bags,
sugar, sugar, bags of sugar, still, ready made bags, sugar, sugar, bags of sugar, still,
ready made bags, sugar, sugar, bags of sugar, still, ready made bags,
sugar, sugar, bags of sugar, still, ready made bags, sugar, sugar, bags of sugar, still,
ready made bags, sugar,

sugar, sugar, bags of sugar,
sugar, sugar, bags of sugar, still, ready made bags,

sugar,
sugar, bags of sugar,
still, ready made bags, sugar,
sugar,
bags of sugar, still, ready made bags,
negroes, negroes, here yet to be made, the negroes came here ready made.
sugar, sugar, bags of sugar,
still, ready made bags,
sugar, sugar, bags of sugar, still,
ready made bags,
sugar, sugar, bags of sugar, still,
ready made bags,
sugar,
sugar, bags of sugar, still, ready made bags
sugar, sugar,
bags of sugar, still,

sugar, bags of sugar, still, ready made bags,
sugar, sugar, bags of sugar, still, ready made bags, sugar, sugar, bags of sugar, still,
ready made bags, sugar, sugar, bags of sugar, still, ready made bags,
sugar, sugar, bags of sugar, still, ready made bags, sugar, sugar, bags of sugar, still,
sugar, sugar, bags of sugar, still,
ready made bags, sugar, sugar, bags of sugar,
still, ready made bags, sugar, sugar, bags of sugar,
still, ready made bags,
sugar, sugar, bags of sugar, still, ready made bags, sugar, sugar,
bags of sugar, still, ready made bags, sugar, sugar, bags of sugar, still, ready made bags,
sugar, sugar, bags of sugar, still, ready made bags, sugar, sugar,
bags of sugar, still, ready made bags, sugar, sugar, bags of sugar, still, ready made bags,
sugar, sugar, bags of sugar, still, ready made bags, sugar, sugar, bags of sugar, still, ready made bags,
sugar, sugar, bags of sugar, still, ready made bags,
sugar, sugar, bags of sugar, still, ready made bags, sugar, sugar, bags of sugar, still,
ready made bags, sugar, sugar, bags of sugar, still, ready made bags,
sugar, sugar, bags of sugar, still, ready made bags, sugar, sugar, bags of sugar, still,
ready made bags, sugar, sugar, bags of sugar, still, ready made bags,
sugar, sugar, bags of sugar, still, ready made bags, sugar, sugar, bags of sugar, still, ready made bags, sugar,
sugar, bags of sugar, still, ready made bags,
sugar, sugar, bags of sugar, still, ready made bags, sugar, sugar, bags of sugar, still, ready made bags, sugar, sugar,
bags of sugar, still, ready made bags,
sugar, sugar, bags of sugar, still, ready made bags, sugar, sugar, bags of sugar, still, ready made bags,
sugar, sugar, bags of sugar, still, ready made bags,
sugar, sugar, bags of sugar, still, ready made bags, sugar, sugar, bags of sugar,
still, ready made bags,
sugar, sugar, bags of sugar, still, ready made bags,
sugar, sugar, bags of sugar, still, ready made bags, sugar,
sugar, bags of sugar, still, ready made bags, sugar, sugar, bags of sugar,
still, ready made bags, bags of sugar, negroes, negroes, here yet to be made,
the negroes came here ready made.
sugar, sugar, bags of sugar, still, ready made bags, sugar, sugar, bags of sugar, still, ready made bags,
sugar, sugar, bags of sugar, still, ready made bags, bags of sugar, negroes, negroes, here yet to be made,
the negroes came here ready made.
sugar, sugar, bags of sugar, still, ready made bags, sugar,
sugar, bags of sugar, still, ready made bags, sugar, sugar, bags of sugar, still, ready made bags,
sugar, sugar, bags of sugar, still, ready made bags, sugar, sugar, bags of sugar, still, ready made bags, sugar,
sugar, bags of sugar, still, ready made bags,
sugar, sugar, bags of sugar, still, ready made bags, sugar, sugar, bags of sugar,
still, ready made bags, sugar, sugar, bags of sugar, still, ready made bags,
bags of sugar, negroes, negroes, here yet to be made,
the negroes came here ready made.
sugar, sugar, bags of sugar, still, ready made bags, sugar, sugar, bags of sugar, still, ready made bags,
sugar, sugar, bags of sugar, still, ready made bags,

SUSAN LEWIS

walking tall

I wouldn't change
my colour for anything

We were just used
as rape machines

We are powerful We are powerful
We are powerful We are powerful
We are powerful
We are powerful We are powerful
We are powerful

We are beautiful
beautiful
beautiful
beautiful

beautiful

why

why

why   why
why
why   why why
why
why   why why us
why
why   why why us

why
why   why
why   why why
why why us
why
why   why why why us

why us

why
why   why
why   why why
why
why   why why us
why
why us   why why

a lot of soul
a lot of soul
a lot of soul a lot of soul a lot of soul
a lot of soul
a lot of soul
a lot of soul a lot of soul
a lot of soul
a lot of soul
a lot of soul   a lot of soul
a lot of soul
a lot of soul
a lot of soul

We've got life, passion
and a lot of soul

SUSAN LEWIS

We were never meant to survive
We've got life, passion
and a lot of soul

Its a hard life and some of us die   some of us die
                                                          some of us die
                                                        some of us die
                                                some of us die some of us die
                                                          some of us die
                        some of us die
                                                              some of us die
                                                          some of us die

                                                                    We are beautiful

        die   die   die   die die die
                        die   die die die
                                        die
die
        die   die   die
                                        die die die   die   die

                        die
                        die
                        die
        die   We are beautiful   die die die
        die   die   die
        die   beautiful
                                                    beautiful
                                                    beautiful   beautiful

                                            die   die

    a lot of soul
            a lot of soul
a lot of soul a lot of soul a lot of soul
            a lot of soul
a lot of soul

    We are powerful We are powerful
                    We are powerful

        die   die   die die die
die   die   die
        die   die

SUSAN LEWIS

SuAndi is a Manchester-based poet,
performer and cultural activist.

Since 1985 she has performed her poetry at national and
international venues and festivals.
Recently introducing a visual
language to her work, she has
developed several highly-structured
performance works able to convey
in more than just words the
difficulties and legacy of straddling
two very distinct worlds.

Recent live works include:
The Story of M (an ICA Live Arts
Commission, 1994) and *This Is
All I've Got To Say* (1993).

She regularly leads educational
workshops and community-based
initiatives, recently organising
ArtBlackLive, a conference and
commissioned programme held
in Manchester. She has curated
several visual art exhibitions and
completed several consultancies.
Her poetry has been published in
numerous anthologies, publications
and journals. Most recent work
includes *There Will Be No Tears,
Nearly Forty* and *Style*.

She is the Cultural Director of Black
Arts Alliance and a member of many
boards including North West Arts
Board, Akwaaba Pan European
Women Network and Black Women
in Europe. She has attended
numerous conferences in the UK, US,
Ghana, Belgium, Germany, Jamaica
and Trinidad as a speaker and
performer.

Photos: Robert Taylor. Thanks to Nana Akua my Ebo Sistah (sic) Catherine Ugwu for inviting me to contribute to this publication; Lois Keidan for her encouragement whilst at the Arts Council of Great Britain and continuous support at the ICA; Michael McMillan for his phone calls telling me to work/rest/work/rest; Tracy Vidal for being my nurse in The Story of M and Rachel Shipp for technical advice. Special thanks for the present and future to Joel Talbert and Keith Antar Mason for private times that result in professional development.

SUANDI

BNP **BLACK NATURAL PALAVER**

Palaver - Conference; prolonged discussion between Africans and other *natives;* profuse or idle talk; affair; business; talk profusely.

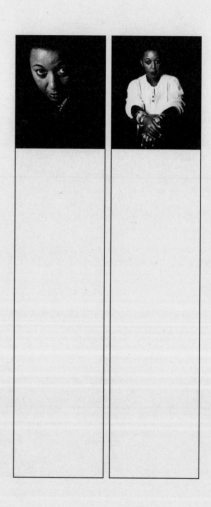

The naive might think my poise Flamenco. It is pure Samba. My left leg firm, the right bent at the knee with my body weight resting on the ball of my foot. My arms, curved at the elbow folding down to the gathered swirls of skirt that I grasp and hoist secure to my hips. I throw my head back, tossing imaginary waves of resplendent curls and sing.

I like to be in America. OK by me in America.

The darkness is sudden, taking with it the image, the dream, of what for me a child aged young, was my first glorious witnessing of something near Black.

Yet America was for me a cinemascope lifestyle where Black people shuffle and Yes Ma'am their way through the story line. I wanted, needed more of that which has been ridiculed, marketed and exploited. That something, which can make an audience moan in understanding. That little piece of magic called Soul.

So why West Side Story? Puerto Ricans were not exactly my next of kin or were they? Wasn't there something in their stories, their love of music, dancing, life, that spoke to me - that small child in the depths of a flea pit cinema - that said, 'Look at this, take a piece for yourself.'

Small wonder that at my next ballet class it was announced that anyone found dancing in the style of the film would be expelled. Hey, Puerto Ricans were family. Distant cousins maybe, but family all the same.

From two to fourteen I had sweated through tap and ballet encouraged by a mother who had never learnt to swing her hips. Just as I was getting tempted by the hullabaloo of rock & roll and smuggled calypsos, just when five hours per week of pink tights and leotards were being forsaken for twisting, Modern Dance was added to the curriculum. Too late for me. Out on my ear, I had out-grown teacher's patience. Why did my hips roll seductively? Who taught my feet that strange sort-of-tribal beat? No longer a girl, this woman was part-grown and the world was destined to get a piece.

For the next few years I busied myself with a varied agenda of boys, a little school work and music, the only source of Blackness around.

1980, in memory of my mother and in the absence of any other means I wrote a thick manuscript intended for my children, the ones that never came. Now and again it was passed to non-blood-family and trusted friends who wanted more, much more of this unfinished tomb of life.

I kept writing and poetry became my skill and in time my full time profession, and although now published, fame-on-the-page didn't tempt, but performance poetry did. It took me right back to the Latino chat of the roof tops where my real appreciation had begun.

There were nine years of self-love, rantings against racism and the Black voice inna-de-wilderness. Then one day in downtown Greenwich New York I met forty million angry people captured by Carrie Mae Weems in photographs and text: *The Voice of My People*. My people. The people of the Diaspora. Working carefully along the edge of the exhibition leaflet I wrote *This Is All I've Got To Say*, my first live art production.

It wasn't bad. Really it wasn't bad at all. What was even better was that as soon as I finished it I was ready for more.

I lie here actually. It wasn't my first solo performance. I had already, unknowingly, produced two other live art collaborations. In *Storia*, a Black Arts Alliance production, the visual artists were at first offended that I wanted their work to backdrop the performance. They were artists they told me, not stage set painters. But they came up with the goods. Like *TIAIGTS* it wasn't a one hundred percent success but I had latched onto something special.

I began to study on it. Some performances held my interest, many barely kept my attention. Live art? They were mainly performances of profanity. I saw more exposed flesh than a day on the beach though not burnt red and peeling. Seems that for reasons I failed to comprehend breasts fell (no that's an exaggeration) breasts peeped out and bums glared like the sick expressions of a BNP marcher. This was not for me.

But occasionally understanding of a style or format inspired me to copy. That is after all what inspiration is based upon. The copying, changing, developing and evolving. These times were only when the artist stopped being a performer and gave a little of themselves. The most interesting stories in the world are our own.

As a Mixed Race, first generation Nigerian daughter, my life stories are full of pictures, some pure in content, images of Black contemporary history that will never rest in academic volumes. Not for me the dank smell of printer's ink, the only time when black lies on top of white with permanency, yet still fearing the wrath and destruction of fire.

Not for me the cold stillness of a gallery where silence is *in situ* and floorboards creak as intruders cross the expanse of no-man's land to no-man's territory. Not for me the choice between gold leaf of colonialism or clip frames held still by steel clips.

Not for me a record label my voice hued in digital transmission to be re-mixed like an old coat with new trimmings of technology that crass my vocal cords into robotic rhythms.

My life has been full of living and so my work must be, has to be, the same. My stories are so similar to your stories with different beginnings, different endings brought about by different characters in different passages of time. To be the same yet different is surely what humanity is about. And humanity only exists when it is live.

This fusion allows me to write from images created by others, to weave them together, not in a demonic-witch style, but with a caring that comes from having to grasp rare opportunities. Not to have a voice, but to have that voice listened to and occasionally understood. This coming together of my skill with other skills has lifted me from the rubbing out of words that do not fit the description to deeds that do.

For me this is the basis of my performance. This is my art and this art is live.

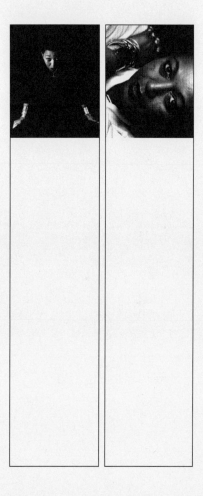

Dan Kwong

Susan Lewis

SuAndi

Reza Abdoh

Elia Arce
Reza Abdoh

Chila Kumari Burman
Elia Arce

Chila Kumari Burman
Ronald Fraser-Munro

Guillermo Gómez-Peña
Ronald Fraser-Munro

Reza Abdoh

Kif Higgins

Elia Arce

Chila Kumari Burman
Kif Higgins

Rhodessa Jones
Ronald Fraser-Munro

Guillermo Gómez-Peña
Rhodessa Jones

Dan Kwong
Dan Kwong

Kif Higgins
Susan Lewis
Susan Lewis

Guillermo Gómez-Peña
SuAndi

Rhodessa Jones
Reza Abdoh
SuAndi
Elia Arce

Dan Kwong
Chila Kumari Burman

Susan Lewis

Ronald Fraser-Munro

SuAndi
Guillermo Gómez-Peña

Kif Higgins

Rhodessa Jones

PERFORMANCE AND THE POWER OF THE POPULAR
Coco Fusco

It can finally be said that the image America projects of itself abroad through its arts is one that reflects the heterogeneity of its population, and the variety of regionalisms that give our culture its particular character. One should not, however, take this to mean that inequities and tensions have been eliminated by the fact of our presence. It is not a harmonious image of diversity that travels to other lands, but one of stridency and conflict, of people who in the eyes of some don't want to 'fit in', so to speak, and of others who are ambivalent about having to inhabit a country with human beings they perceive as unlike them. I begin this essay two years after the PC backlash against multiculturalism chilled activist efforts in the cultural sector, and just a few weeks after the passing of Proposition 187 in California which fuelled right-wing nativism and gave racist anti-immigrant agitators a new sense of legitimacy. In other words, we may be here, but there are powerful forces at work in our country to destabilise our sense of being here to stay.

Although no thorough survey of performance art of the past decade can reasonably overlook the contributions of artists of colour, there is no consensus as to the significance of our increased visibility. Our presence has been read as a sign of the milieu's 'new' cultural diversity, but our entry and the postmodernist debates that encircle us have also been associated with the dismantling of hierarchical categories that set 'high art' performance apart from other performative practices of vernacular cultures, which - for some - signals the end of performance as an artform. More than a few contemporary performance artists of colour have pointed to the racist implications of suggesting that our engagement with an artform might coincide with its death. At the same time, our

More than a few contemporary performance artists of colour have pointed to the racist implications of suggesting that our engagement with an artform might coincide with its death.

relation to the popular is not a given. We *do* wrestle with its power. Some embrace and reinterpret popular forms as a mode of aesthetic experimentation, while others eschew them as bad taste or as tainted by commercialism; nonetheless, we must all contend with its being here to stay. In its industrialised form, popular culture is a formidable shaper of public consciousness that relies heavily on the display of subaltern performativity to convey its messages. In the more grass-roots versions lie the styles, sounds and attitudes that mark the difference of our cultural identities from those of the mainstream.

The spectre of the popular and the stereotype of the exotic entertainer loom large as part of an historical legacy that shapes the reception of 'culturally diverse' work in the US and Europe. Questioning our ties to that history is not new; in fact, the issue of how artists of colour relate to popular culture and to racial stereotypes has been central since the Harlem Renaissance, when Langston Hughes celebrated black vernacular, and later recited his verse to a jazz beat. Leading theorist of the period Alain Locke called on artists to look to popular and ancestral traditions for inspiration: it would take, however, more than a decade before such visual artists as Jacob Lawrence would begin to take on such a challenge in a truly innovative manner. In fact, more than a few visual artists at the onset of the Harlem Renaissance opted in favour either of creating very academic-looking paintings and sculptures to distinguish themselves from 'Africana', or adopting the neo-primitive styles celebrated by early European moderns in an entirely uncritical manner. Similar dynamics have emerged in every debate about the role of culture in movements for social change and which styles best 'reflect' or represent the life and spirit of a community and a culture. These were some of the key influences that led up to the

multicultural performance 'boom' of the 1980s and 90s, which I outline so as to shed
light on the more significant trends in multicultural performance art and their relation to
notions of the popular today.

It is generally understood that performance as a term was introduced in the early 1970s
to describe art that was ephemeral, time-based and process oriented, that incorporated
the body as an object and as a subject of inquiry, and explored extreme forms of
behaviour, cultural taboos, and social issues[1]. It is also used retroactively to refer to the
art movements that are often seen as having led up to it; the happenings and intermedia
experiments of the 1960s, the Black Mountain College group of the 1950s, Dadaist and
Surrealist events of the 20s and 30s, and so on. This genealogy is flagrantly Eurocentric,
and lends credence to the assumption that American artists of colour started doing
performance thanks to multicultural policies in the 1980s. While many artists of colour
working in performance have been influenced by the work of the aforementioned
twentieth century avant-garde movements, a more complete understanding of their
approaches and styles needs to take into account a host of other factors.

Performance by artists of colour in the US takes place against the historical backdrop of
the subjection of subaltern cultures to centuries of regulation and economic exploitation
by outsiders. Africans brought to the United States as slaves had their principal
performative tool - the drum - taken from them. Many performative acts in black
communities were forced into secrecy as a strategy of survival. Several Native American
dances and performative rituals were outlawed as part of a larger 'civilising' project that
went hand in hand with the conquest of the American West. Some of those prohibitions
were not lifted until the early 1970s. From the late nineteenth century onward, these
attempts at subaltern social control coincided with the commodification of black and
native performance for white mass entertainment, and with the sardonic mimicry of
racial stereotypes in the form of, for example, the black-faced minstrel. As a result, a split
was forged between subaltern performance for insiders and outsiders, and between
patterns of reception for each group.

These historical factors established patterns that continue to this day. For example, many

Pages 162 & 163
Jimmie Durham
The East London
Coelacanth (1993-4)
Photos: Maria Thereza Alves

of the critiques of Jennie Livingston's 1991 documentary about black and Latino voguers, *Paris is Burning*, were directed quite pointedly at the filmmaker's economic and voyeurist exploitation of the voguers and their performative subculture, and were cast quite self-consciously in light of the history to which I have alluded[2]. It is also part of the legacy of these prohibitions and of the internalisation of racist notions of aesthetic value that the 'authenticity' of our work continues to be measured against the most reductive and stereotypical notions of the popular. For example, black conceptual artist Adrian Piper does not focus on the famed orality of African-American culture and as a result is often labelled 'less black' than those who do. And the *Two Undiscovered Amerindians* performance that Guillermo Gómez-Peña and myself carried out in 1992 generated enormous controversy for audiences and sponsoring institutions precisely because we were not 'real' representatives of the culture we displayed.

Chronologies of the history of performance art that begin in Europe, rarely, if ever, acknowledge the importance that direct and indirect contact with non-western performers played in giving shape to early twentieth century avant garde artists' concepts of aesthetic transgression. The early modernist interest in performative practices of non-western cultures as keys that could unlock the Western unconscious and offer alternatives to realism and classicism has informed nearly every subsequent form of performance art in the US[3]. Even the contemporary trend of tattooing, piercing and scarification in performance art by white artists relies to some extent on stereotypes of 'primitive ritual', retracing the steps of the Dadaists. This history has led to a certain protectiveness in subaltern communities about what cultural practices can be shown to whom, and has generated anxieties about the exhibitionist quality of performance art. It has also encouraged many artists to focus specifically on the dynamics of objectification and exoticisation of people of colour by mainstream American society. Artists dealing with these issues often adopt the strategy of reworking cultural stereotypes, a very different objective from that of the imaginative retrieval of 'original cultural forms', or that of creating entirely new paradigms devoid of historical traces. Reworking stereotypes leads to heated debates about the extent to which the artists' ironic reinterpretation of an established paradigm can be discerned by different audiences, and hence the danger of

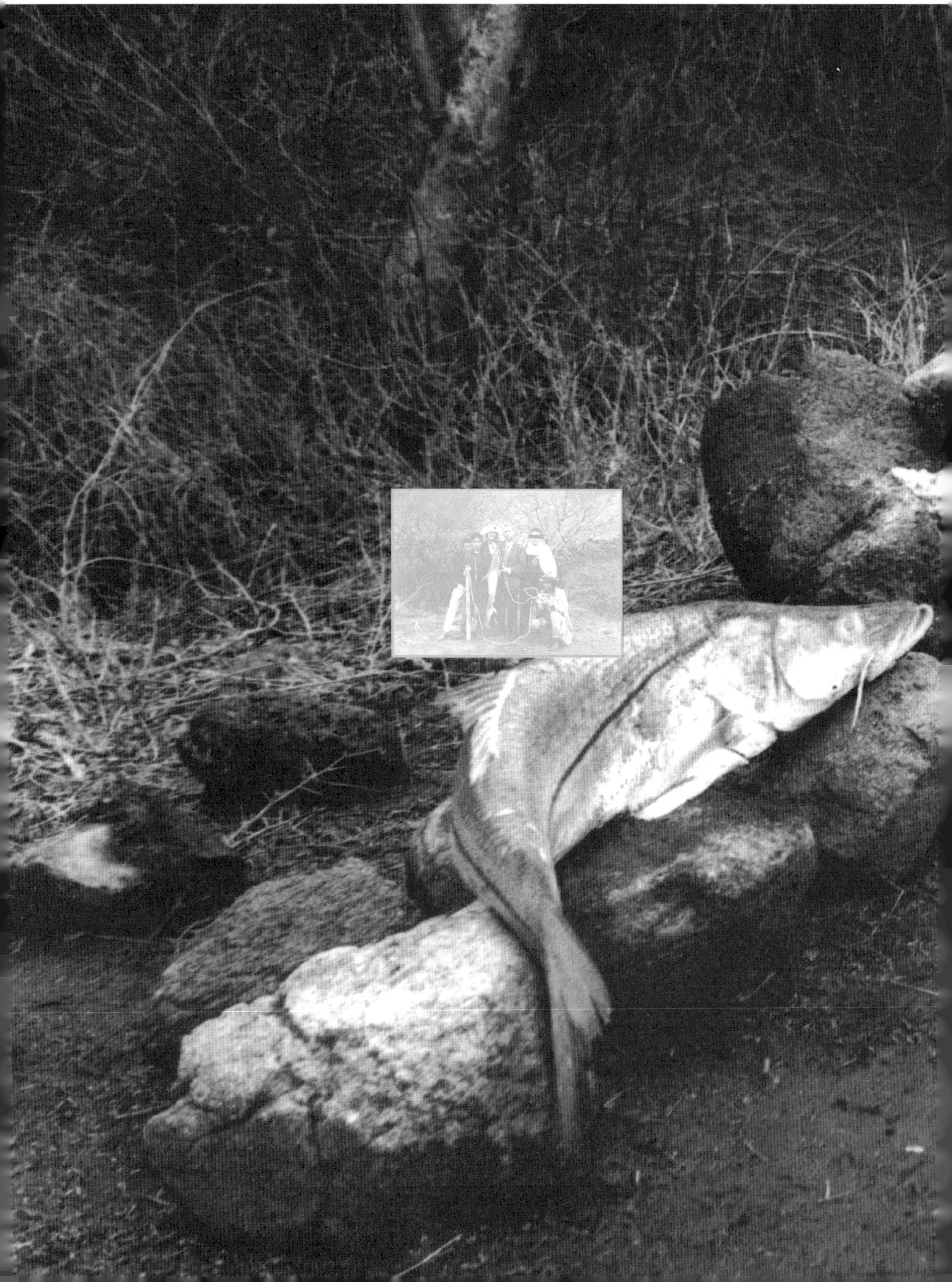

inadvertently recapitulating the scenarios they seek to subvert.

Performance artists of colour in the US also draw on a wealth of culturally specific practices in addition to the contributions of twentieth century European and white American avant gardes. While the presumably intrinsic performativity of the subaltern body is still fetishised by white artists, many dancer/performers of colour such as Urban Bush Women, David Rousseve and Merian Soto have focused their work largely on recontextualising popular dance forms. Another one of the influences that has most affected artists of colour in the US is the history of vernacular performance-poetry and storytelling in subaltern communities as the primary mode of transmitting unofficial histories and of defining vernacular style. For African-Americans, the performer-prototype is the *griot* storyteller. Many native traditions have a similar trickster figure, who knows all and can manoeuvre effortlessly around any obstacle set for him. That figure is often invoked by Jimmie Durham in his performances, as well as in the fictitious anthropologies and the characters he creates for his installation work.

With the flowering of regionalism and community arts movements in the 1980s, dozens of performers working in the storytelling mode came to the fore in the US, and were promoted by such venues as North Carolina's Alternate Roots. For Chicanos, an equivalent rural archetype was the balladeer with his/her *corrido*, a song designed to preserve a community's legends. The urban counterpart was the *pachuco*, a street-wise mover and shaker who, through bilingual word play, could always outsmart the law. This smooth-talking king of the urban jungle was also invoked by such Nuyorican poets of the early 1970s as Miguel Piñiero and Miguel Algarín. In the late 1980s and 90s, as performance-poetry was galvanised around the reconstituted Nuyorican Poets Cafe in New York's Loisaida, that figure became current again. While these types tend to be cast as male, feminist artists and critics have taken note of their female counterparts. Lowery Sims, for example, notes that the confrontational tone of many black women performance artists' monologues retraces the culturally specific expressive strategy of 'acting out', a forceful union of body language and energetic commentary deployed by black women in response to provocation[4].

The invocation of these figures carries with it a concept of art and community that allows artists to reconstitute non-European cultural traditions. In her analysis of African-American artist Faith Ringgold's use of masks and quilts in performances in the mid 1970s, Lowery Sims suggests that Ringgold and many other black artists give their art objects a function in their performances as a way to reclaim African tradition[5]. Such evocation of a shared past is also the strategy of 'naming' a community as the ideological dimension of progressive political struggle. Artists and activists draw on a history of symbolic action as a catalyst for ethnic self-empowerment. Among the more prominent examples from this history is the Free Southern Theatre, led by John O'Neal. An integrated ensemble founded at Tougalou College in 1963 in Mississippi by Freedom Movement activists, the group developed a variety of works dealing with racism and the recovery of black cultural forms. Another key example is Teatro Campesino, founded by Luis Valdez in California in 1965. Valdez recruited his actors among striking farm workers and developed political performances that were carried out at picket lines. Some years later, in the early 1970s, the Sacramento based art group Royal Chicano Air Force would take up hit-and-run dramatic actions to draw attention to Mexican farmworker-led boycotts, while Chicano artist Rene Yañez carried out street performances in San Francisco's Mission District. Contemporary African-American artist Keith Antar Mason and his group, The Hittite Empire, carry on this tradition by developing performances out of dialogues with young black men about topical issues such as the Los Angeles insurrection, and the case of the young black men who were tried for the rape of the white corporate executive in New York's Central Park.

Performance art's frequent inquiry into the relationship between artist, artwork and audience, and the preference many performance artists have shown for presenting their work outside the domain of arts institutions, have led to its frequent characterisation as more democratic in spirit than other art forms, and better suited to the consciousness-raising function that many progressive social movements have proscribed for radical art. Part of that task has been to bring the experiences of those living far from the mainstream into the arts arena. The ongoing interest in incorporating non-professionals, such as the homeless men (mostly of colour) of the Los Angeles Poverty Department, or in working with oral histories, as did Robbie McCauley in her performance projects dealing with memories of racial conflicts over bussing in Boston and voter registration in Mississippi, are strategies that stem from that populist view of the function of performance art. That engagement with the social is also evident in the ways that artists carrying out site-specific performances have shifted the political emphasis of such work away from the critique of galleries and art commodification that was widespread in the 1970s to the social and historical significance of sites. Hence, in the 80s the interracial Border Art Workshop/El Taller de Arte Fronterizo claimed the US-Mexico border as a laboratory for experimenting with intercultural relations and engaging in performances that were specifically designed to transgress the laws that divide the two countries and peoples.

In spite of the strength of these performative interventions outside the gallery system, it would be a mistake to reduce all truly culturally diverse performance to politically engaged collectives operating outside arts institution. Much of performance since the 1960s has explored the body, its limits and capabilities, and its social codification. These lines of inquiry easily lent themselves to the concerns of feminism and of artists examining the processes of racial classification, and ethnic marking of different bodies. As early as 1964, Fluxus member Yoko Ono performed *Cut Piece* in Japan and New York, in which she asked her audience to cut her clothing to pieces. This work has often been interpreted as a revelation of the individual's capacity for violence against others, and even as an indirect comment on the Vietnam War. In 1966, Puerto Rican artist Rafael Montañez Ortiz began to create performances involving animal sacrifice, destroying musical instruments and developing fictional archeologies that combined his studies of non-Western rituals with his background in Abstract Expressionism.

In the early 1970s much performance pushed the inquiries of the 60s further, dealing with the testing of physical limits and social taboos. The period coincides with the emergence of Adrian Piper, an indisputable pioneer known for her extraordinary formal rigour and her ability to bring social issues of racism and racial classification to bear on conceptualist practices. For her early performance series *Mythic Being* (1972-1975), in which she engaged in various forms of anti-social behaviour in public and tested audience responses, Piper impersonated an inner-city black male wearing an afro wig,

*Turf: A Conversational
Concert in Black and White*
**by Robbie MaCaulay
in association with
The Arts Company**
Cambridge,
Massachusetts (1993)
Photo: Jay R Phillips, courtesy
of The Arts Company

Yoko Ono
Cut Piece **(1964)**
Photo courtesy of
Leono Photo Archive

Nao Bustamente
Indigerito **(1994)**
Photo: D Oviedo

Lorraine O'Grady
Mlle Bourgeois
Noire Goes to the
New Museum (1981)
Photo: Coreen Simpson

Papa Colo
Superman 51 (1977)
Photo courtesy of Exit
Art, New York

Guillermo Gómez-Peña
and Roberto Sifuentes
The Temple of Confessions
(1994)
Photo: Dirk Bakker

dark glasses and a moustache. Critic Judith Wilson describes her work as investigating 'social-versus-self perceptions, the construction of identity and functions of difference.'[6] Interestingly, while the focus of her actions was on exploring her *Mythic Being* as an 'emblem of alien confrontation', the specific character she adopted allowed her to inhabit the identity of a working class, visibly black male, the personification of a community from which her own social position, education and light complexion distanced her.

Piper would go on to transfer her *Mythic Being* to two-dimensional pieces, to explore the racial fears and guilt complexes of white viewers, and to use her self-portraits and personal history as a means of exploring racial stereotypes. In her 1983-85 performances of *Funk Lessons*, Piper deployed a combination of lecturing on the nature of funk music and live demonstrations involving her audiences. Bringing her audiences' anxieties about a popular black musical form to the surface, Piper sought to analyse the racially codified and highly elitist appraisal by white critics and artists of her prior use of 'popular' funk music in 'high art' installations as having 'cheapened' her material[7].

Other performance artists of colour working in the 1970s were also exploring the sense of alienation and displacement that being perceived as undesirable, foreign, or uprooted might engender. The late Ana Mendieta began undertaking poetic actions in 1972 in Iowa, dealing first with violence against women, and then with her exile from Cuba. Her performances, usually presented in photo documentation form, represent her longing for homeland in the form of portraits of herself in positions that establish a ritualised connection to the earth. In San Francisco, the late Korean artist Theresa Hak Kyung-Cha began creating performances in 1974 with *Barren Cave Mute* in which she launched her exploration of the theme of detachment from language as a structure of communication. In Los Angeles, the Chicano collective ASCO (Harry Gamboa, Gronk, Pattsi Valdez and Willie Herrón) performed street actions called *No Movies* (intended for, but never reaching, film) about their experiences as members of an urban Latino underclass. During this same period New York-based artists such as David Hammons, Houston Conwill and Papo Colo were undertaking performative actions as a means of breaking with artistic conventions and engaging with social issues.

The increasing use in the 80s of autobiographical material shifted the performance agenda to the voicing of subjectivities that had been repressed or marginalised by enforced societal norms. This applied as much to the issue of diversity in the arts as it did to the recognition of multiple voices and ideological divisions within subaltern communities. For example, while black cultural debates of the 1970s were heavily influenced by the spirit of cultural nationalism, the intervention of feminist critiques in the late 70s and 80s brought a radical revision of that perspective. In 1980 Lorraine O'Grady created *Mlle Bourgeoise Noire* to the New York arts milieu, a satirical take on the assimilationist aspirations and sexist values of the black middle class. O'Grady would be followed by Baltimore-based artists Joyce Scott and Kay Lawal who created the *Thunder Thigh Review*, a performance critique of stereotypical femininity from the perspective of overweight women. During the same period, San Francisco-based artist Rhodessa Jones challenged black artist's reticence toward nudity and exhibitionism with a look at the lives of erotic dancers in *The Legend of Lilly Overstreet*.

This desire to break down sexual taboos is not limited to women dealing with the conventions of black femininity. More recently, the interest in sexual prohibition as a means of control has broadened to explore homosexual, lesbian and transgendered sexualities. Gay male performance poet Essex Hemphill and the group Pomo Afro Homos, for example, addresses such issues as homoerotic desire and homophobia in the black community. Japanese-American performance artist Denise Uyehara looks at stereotypes of Asian female sexuality from a lesbian perspective in her piece *Hello Sex Kitty*. Post-punk Chicano artist Nao Bustamente blends and pushes cultural and transgender themes to parodic extremes in recent work such as *Indigerito*, which involves her strapping a burrito to her genital area as a dildo and inviting her audience to take bites out of it.

From the beginning of the 80s to the present, the themes of gender politics, institutionalised racism in the arts and the formation of hybrid cultures and identities have dominated the work of emergent performance artists of colour. The performance monologue movement of the 1980s served as an ideal arena for the exploration of subaltern identity through poetic testimony, using stories that dramatised the dilemma of cross-cultural misunderstanding. Guillermo Gómez-Peña's chronicle of his transformation from Mexico City youth to bicultural immigrant, *Border Brujo*, is among the best-known performance pieces of this genre. Dan Kwong's *Samurai Center Fielder,* Alina Troyano's *Carmelita Tropicana,* and the skits created by the performance comedians of Culture Clash and Chicano Secret Service also celebrate the experience of life in the space between cultures through the creation of self-consciously hybrid and/or parodic characters. Though the majority of this work is intended to subvert notions of a nation built on a singular cultural identity, some artists recognise that there are moments when a satirical simulation of absolute assimilation can be an effective comic strategy. In the midst of the political and racial tension caused by California's Proposition 187, for example, Chicano Secret Service member Lalo Lopez reinvented himself as Daniel D. Portado (Spanish for 'deported Daniel'), and launched an organisation called Hispanics for Wilson, which landed him an invitation to be a guest on a Spanish language television talk show about governor Pete Wilson's agenda. His true identity was never revealed.

One of the most hotly-debated multicultural issues in the arts has been around institutionalised racism and cultural appropriation. Several artists have engaged in performative projects that have dissected the role that cultural institutions and the discourses of anthropology and art history have played in reproducing colonialist modes of objectifying non-western cultures. The very fact that so much of the art and artefacts of non-western culture continue to be exhibited in natural history museums along with flora, fauna and animal life as evidence of Western man's domination of the 'natural' world through scientific knowledge is a testimony to a racist legacy. Luiseño artist James Luna has been creating performances that dramatically illustrate the relationship between white cultural institutions and native cultures since the mid-1980s. For his *Artifact Piece* (1985), Luna donned a simple loincloth and lay motionless in a glass case at San Diego's Museum of Man, where he was on exhibit for several days. Adjacent cases displayed his identification papers and personal effects as artefacts of his culture. Luna often recalls in his description of the piece how spectators would poke and pinch him to determine if he was in fact real and alive - a sad comment on how effectively our cultural institutions have ingrained in us the idea that indigenous cultures are obsolete by presenting human

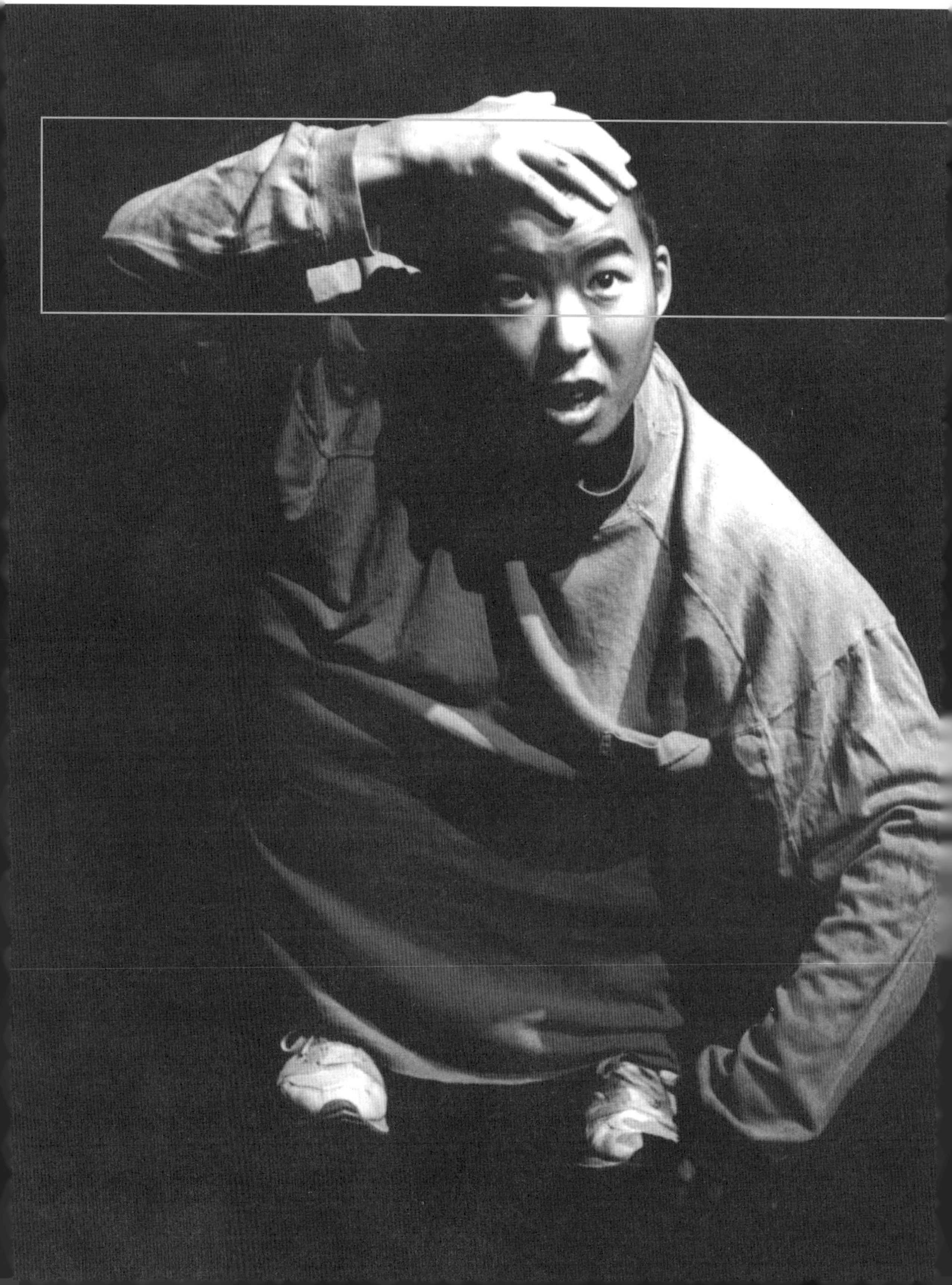

Denise Uyehara
*Headless Turtleneck
Relatives*
Photo: Chuck Stallard

Carmelita Tropicana
*Memories of the
Revolution* (1987)
Photo: Dona Ann McAdams

Carmelita Tropicana
Live at a PS122 benefit
New York (1989)
Photo: Dona Ann McAdams

remains and artists as vestiges of a dead culture. Some of my own collaborations with Guillermo Gómez-Peña have explored similar issues. In our travelling performance, *Two Undiscovered Amerindians Visit...* (1992-94), in which we exhibited ourselves as the inhabitants of an island in the Gulf of Mexico, and were often mistaken for 'real savages', we sought to make a satirical commentary on the ethnographic display of non-westerners for white audiences, and the commodification of ethnicity as consumable exotica for contemporary cultural institutions.

Historically a haven for renegades from conventional art forms, performance has, over the past three decades, become a territory increasingly dominated by those most often excluded from them: women and people of colour. In recent years it has also become perhaps the most productive arena in the arts for challenging the boundaries between art and politics, as artists have used performative strategies in response to such social crises as homelessness, the AIDS epidemic, domestic violence and systemic racism. In addition, the reliance that non-commercial alternative cultural venues supporting performance have had on government funding and the right-wing backlash against the arts as a decadent, corrupting force, have led to performance becoming the prime area for debating the relationship between art, artists and the state. Given the censorship scandals of recent years and the ephemeral quality of the medium, performance has taken on a reputation for being trouble incarnate for the status quo; yet another version of the paranoid view of American society as brimming with enemies within. Seen at one time as a genre that allowed artists to eschew their status as object makers, to test their minds and bodies and explore extreme behaviour, the artform has become a stage for the presentation of cultural and sexual difference, issues that mainstream society has pushed to the margins. I would not, however, explain the character of performance today on the basis of what is repressed in other areas of the social. Despite the often racist ways in which the relationship has been characterised, performance has historically been and continues to be about the unconscious, both individual and collective. It is about how meanings are generated in the moment, out of interactions between individuals and between cultures. It is as much concerned with what we can control about our identities as what we cannot. This territory of multiple perceptions, and of the unpredictable, is a perfect place from which to continue to test the limits of the promise of democracy and tolerance: great ideas to which this country aspires, but which it has such tremendous difficulties actually living up to.

1   See Robyn Brentano's 'Outside the Frame: Performance, Art and Life', in *Outside the Frame: Performance and the Object, A Survey History of Performance Art in the USA since 1950*, Cleveland Center for Contemporary Art, Ohio, 1994

2   See for example Marcos Becquer and Jose Gatti's 'Elements of Vogue' in Third Text No. 16/17, Autumn/Winter, 1991, and bell hooks' 'Is Paris Burning?' in *Black Looks: Race and Representation*, South End Press, Boston, 1992

3   Coco Fusco, 'The Other History of Intercultural Performance' in The Drama Review No. 38, 1 (T141), Spring, 1994.

4   Lowery Sims, 'Aspects of Performance in the Work of Black American Women Artists' in *Feminist Art Criticism, An Anthology*, ed. Arlene Raven, Cassandra Langer and Joanna Freuh, UMI Research Press, Ann Arbor, Michigan, 1988

5   *Ibid.*

6   Judith Wilson, 'In Memory of the News and of Ourselves: The Art of Adrian Piper' in Third Text No.16/17, Autumn/Winter 1991

7   *Ibid.*

REVISIONIST EXAMINATION

Keith Antar Mason

Revisionist Examination

A performance conceived and written by Keith Antar Mason

Character list

White man guest lecturer

Black man in need of education

At rise

(Let's describe the black man in need of education: he is tied to a wooden chair wearing only a pair of black silk boxers. He is spitting up blood and has been badly beaten. He cannot escape and he is mumbling. The boxers should fit very tightly. The fear of his masculinity is the image that is being constructed. He is sitting in an area that is covered with white flour. There is a wooden desk across from him. On top of it is the white man guest lecturer. He is smoking a cigarette and drinking a 40oz. He is wearing only a pair of white long johns and aiming a gun at the ceiling shooting at some unseen target. In the background we faintly hear side one of Young Americans by David Bowie. It plays through the entire event.)

White man guest lecturer

We are not leaving here, until you say it. That David Bowie is the godfather of soul. Damian Williams is guilty ... and likes getting fucked in the ass like Rodney King ... and he should not get a dime of tax payers' money and your black ass is guilty of burning and looting ... you fucking no good nigger bastard.

You looted because your no good ass was too lazy to get a job and earn a living ... you burned down my business and then you set fires in Malibu a year later and Michael

The Hittite Empire
Sexual Illegals
Photo: Jose Ivey

Jackson is a child molester ... you nigger dog. *(He sits up)* Repeat that ... or else ... I am going to come over there and cut your foot off Toby ... I am waiting.

Black man in need of an education
(He leans his head back and looks at the ceiling) I am gonna kill every god-damned slant-eyed gook in this mother-fucking county that told you I looted your place ... then I am going to ride down on every mother-fucking cinco de mayo mother-fucker that is taking my hood from me and leaving me a minority in the minority. I was going home man ... I needed some food on that day ... SHIT ... it was burning ... already ... I went in ... and got some shit ... bread ... milk ... I work man ... I am one of those hard-working niggers ... I knew we ... were going to need ... things.

White man guest lecturer
I owned the gun shop. What did you need in there? Never no turning back ... listen ... homie ... homeboy ... I do not want to hear your blues ... or how you fry chicken ... or why some niggers grow on trees at the end of ropes ... I want you to confess to me like your mother gets down on her knees every Sunday and sucks that white Jesus' dick ... I am not satisfied ... and so you have to pay ... you know that three strikes and you are out: one you are black ... two you got a dick ... three ... you looted and burned down property ... my property ... and we have not re-written the constitution ... no sir that part we have not done ... you have worn me out ... I use to feel for you ... that is why I stayed down in the jungle ... with the bloods ... I use to give a damn ... but then compassion fatigue set in ... now I don't give a fuck about what was going on in that hood ... man to smoke a blunt and hit some black pussy every once in a while ... the thought just gets me harder than

The Hittite Empire
Sexual Illegals
Photo: Jose Ivey

The Hittite Empire
Sexual Illegals
Photo: Jose Ivey

Japanese arithmetic for the blind ... but that is beside the point ... simba. You was supposed to tell them to go to church and pray ... you had a job nigger ... and that is the bargain ... we give you a job ... you are supposed to lick my ass. Sell out and be thankful.

Black man in need of an education
(He screams) I don't want to remember it this way ... my history ... somehow there ain't gonna be no 'national beat a nigga down week' or just a 'beat a nigga down day' ... fuck a National Holiday ... March 3rd any year right? ... 'on planet beat that ass' ... you just gonna turn it into some white version of history aren't you ... 25 years from now ... a nigga like me will be dead ... won't I ... and your old white ass will tell it the way you want it to be ... won't you?

White man guest lecturer
You Blacks, and Hispanics and Koreans just wanted some governmental funding, that's all. It was the end of the Bush era ... yeah yeah ... some seed money for your efforts ... sorta like the Boston Tea Party: George Washington, Patrick Henry and Thomas Paine ... I can see some twisted version of history ... that is what you want me to teach my children right? You are correct. I will not be teaching that nor allowing it to be taught that way.

Black man in need of an education
That is not true ... I think your children know very well that Mr. Brady died of Aids ... that George Washington lied ... and peep this ... as soon as Michael Jackson got on national TV and said he was proud to be an Afrikan in America ... he became a nigger child molester worst than King Kong ... indicted and convicted on Court TV for the entertainment of millions.

White man guest lecturer
(He rushes the black man in need of an education. He puts the gun in his mouth) Damian Williams likes Latino dick up the ass. Say it. *(Takes gun from out of the Black man in need of education's mouth)*

Keith Antar Mason
Photo: Jose Ivey

Black man in need of an education

Iron Malik Tyson knows how brothers are dying in the joint from Aids ... he has read a thousand books now ... bell hooks and Cornel West ... have written powerful essays about his living conditions inside the prison ... and confirmed the belief that jail may be a path to redemption for bad niggas like me and the ones watching this ... but you gonna have to kill me ... to make me say that it was wrong ... for what I did or what any other brother did ... on April 29th 1992 ... it was right to tear down the master's plantation. I have bent over too many times having to put my money up on the counter first before I even ordered anything to let them know I was buying and then was expected to say thank you. And I was the one buying something. Too many times I had to wait even farther away from the ATM to get my money out ... cause I didn't want to freak other people ... white people out ... you know ... I was mistaken for the dope man while working on my PhD in Mythological Studies. And that is when I discovered the power of contemporary myth-making in these times and how it is done ... I am one ... my silk drawers-wearing ass my Mercedes Benz-driving ass was and still is JUST a nigga, huh ... I got to wee-wee man I got to piss ... open your mouth and tell your history. See you go have to kill me, bitch. White pussy-assed mother-fucker. Before I deny what is still going down, bitch.

White man guest lecturer

Okay okay I am going to blow your head off ... after I do that ... I am going to stick my dick - I like that - I am going to stick my dick in what's left of your brains ... 'cause as your people say 'a mind is a terrible thing to waste nigger'. *(The lights started to fade. We hear a gunshot. In the dark we hear the White man guest lecturer fucking the brains of the Black man in need of an education. We then hear him orgasm).*

The end

Sometimes words and images are the only weapons you can take against your oppression.

My imagination is a weapon. I was born a poet but the world I live in demands that I become a holy warrior.

I am a racist playwright because that is what the 'white reviewer' implied with her coded language about *Revisionist Examination*. You have just read it. (She also got the title wrong.) I created a paranoid farce about what it feels like in post-insurrection LA. Blacks are being made to feel guilty because they rebelled about injustice. Everyone has forgotten the words 'not guilty' in relation to the Rodney King trial. And we have moved on to the O J Simpson case anyway.

Sometimes words and images are the only weapons you can take against your oppression. As a black man who is an artist of Afrikan descent living in the United States that is my job. Most of my work directly challenges the effects of racism on my community.

It is important for me to say that my imagination is a weapon. I was born a poet but the world I live in demands that I become a holy warrior.

Daryl H Miller, LA Daily News, 15 September 1993:
Keith Antar Mason is only half joking when he says his new performance piece lacks an intermission because he doesn't want the audience to escape. Working with the Los Angeles-based performing group The Hittite Empire, the 36-year-old writer-director-performer has earned a reputation as someone who makes audiences confront anger, fear, prejudice and desire... He doesn't mince words when criticising what he regards as a racist society, nor does he hold back when blasting the Los Angeles Festival, the very event that commissioned *Sexual Illegals*. In a recent conversation, he went so far as to dismiss the festival - a multicultural blowout that explores Los Angeles' ethnic communities and artists - as nothing more than a curiosity-seeker's tour through other cultures...

I actively seek funding from art supporters in order to present my work to educate my audiences on the effects of racism. This is a political act. The Third Reconstruction of the Afrikan-American Male has been conducted and failed. Now we are hurled backwards to the Fourth Middle Passage and our stories of the war zone need to be told. My future as a free man is being limited right now. My country is building better and smarter prisons so that they can eventually lock me up. This is not paranoia, this is what Governor Wilson is seeking with the Three Strike Laws that have been signed in. The closing of Amerika's mind when it comes to black men in the US is clear. No one is above the law. And the law is made so that they can lock up the next generations of black men. The slave ship is now a prison. Syphilis was used in the latter part of the 15th century, now Aids in the latter part of the 20th century. Black drug sellers get more time locked away in prisons - in conditions that breed the exchange of the Aids virus. Get ready in the early years of the next century to hear about the Nobel prize winner coming from the Amerikan Gulag. Our Drug Czar will be dismayed that the international world could recognise the merit of a black boy, writing from a prison cell, exposing man's cruelty to man. But the Nobel selection will not be enough to win that black boy's release. The laws have already been put on the books. The money will be given to a victim restitution programme. Another way to keep the wealth out of the Afrikan-American community.

The 13th amendment of the US constitution will be used against us. The mainstream white media has made it possible for all Amerikans to believe that all black men are criminals, even their artists. Gangsta Rappers have now become Gangsta Minstrels: politicised revolutionaries selling records, CDs and cassettes. Our images co-opted - even my anger, which is directed at white liberal progressives in the art world who are constantly struggling to build relationships with black artists, then betray their own commitments when they move on to the next hot issue. Life-long working relationships are not a part of the conversation. Nor is the funding: be warned.

Robert Koehler, LA Times, 6 March 1992:
Keith Antar Mason is on his way, which is one reason why he
named his new, sinewy performance work at Highways,
River... Mason has put new muscle into his running theme
of the pain of the black man... A sense of reconciliation
emerges in *River*, with one terrible exception: he states - and

repeats - that 'what Hitler wanted to create was nothing to what we had already set in motion in this country'. Mason's suggestion that the American slave trade of 60 million people outweighed the mass murder of six million Jews (and gays and leftists as well) is morally indefensible and pointlessly divisive of precisely the two groups, blacks and Jews, who were at the front lines of the US Civil Rights movement. It feels like a dare to his audience, and contradicts everything *River* is about.

'Hello, this is John Dickhead, from the Slacker Museum of Corrupted Art. I am interested in presenting your work. In our next BIG festival. The Bad Boys of the Art World. We will fly you in, hotel, commission a work so on and so on ... please call me. I have to get your signature on the grant application by this evening. Thank-you.'

I am not complaining. I use that scenario; I go, and I do the work in most cases. I bring in the Afrikan-American community and I hope that I inform them of where this institution is morally and when the next insurrection occurs please come back here ... remove all the Afrikan artwork stolen in the 18th and 19th centuries and then burn this institution down. A Bloody Cultural War is being waged against us as black men and as artists. We are not losing. We are indeed winning. There are casualties. There always are and there will be in the future.

I sit on panels with the enemy and watch them work the Chinese menu - one from slot A one from slot B and one from slot C. Then their favourite artist is given complete funding. They use this to defend the panel selection process and to defend diversity in the same breath. I am a performance artist making work knowing that this is my reality. The question of artistic merit is a farce here in the States. White and from New York is still number one choice. It is still an old white boys network whether male or female. I still do not know who the old white boys are. I have not had lunch with any of them. My name is not on their tongues. They don't write cheques out for my work. Nor will the Chair of the NEA write a cheque out directly for me. But people of colour will be used to defend the good work of the NEA.

I am a working artist. I live in the Afrikan-American marketplace. I struggle to pay bills and to keep a place to work and live. My work reflects this issue. Right now, I feel it is my mandate to educate and nurture other black male artists throughout my country and in the UK.

I will not allow the imaginations of other young black artists to be turned over to the white art administrators out there struggling to raise funds. I have been sexually harassed by a white female art administrator, because of confusion between what my work is on stage and what I am in real life. I have been fired from Highways Performance Space in LA by a white female art administrator, and hated by the white majority who decided that I was no longer a member of that community because I was not in tune with their agenda. This was immediately following the LA insurrection. I was taking food to people in the Afrikan-American community while Highways wanted me to assuage their guilt. The turnover of people of colour immediately after the insurrection in major and alternative art spaces needs to be examined ... and it is in my work. The rage of those betrayals are warnings. A Bloody Cultural Revolution is in the making. Because a revisionist history is already taking place. When they tell the story of Highways and how things were curated there, they leave my name off the records, and no person of colour sits on the curatorial staff as a paid employee. As an artist I make work based on my personal experiences. I name ... names. And I lose gigs. Art supporters turn their favour to some other coloured person ... these are the images that fill my work with its power. I am not angry without cause. I have a lot of reasons to practice voodoo, don't I?

And that is the work's spiritual truth. Instead of turning over other young black artists I train them to confront their secrets, to struggle with the ideas and dreams and hopes that they have to live with and be artists in their world. We conduct long term residencies - four to six weeks. Their stories are the sacred words ... their images become the holy icons of enlightenment. Our bodies become the ritual workings of the performance. We do not get awarded the big funds. Our culture is within our sweat and tears. Our very survival.

Alexis Greene, Theater Week, 17 August 1992:

Hatred of those in power was also the thrust of The Hittite Empire, a Los Angeles-based group that aims to rivet attention on what its performers experience as the African-American man's fight for life...

One central image of *49 Blues Songs for a Jealous Vampire* became more lame than serious, as Mason, sitting in a chair at the edge of the stage, continually ripped pages out of several books (among them, the Kitty Dukakis autobiography), and harangued white Americans to 'catch up with me' and to recognise that African-American men are human beings. 'How the fuck do you think you're going to ever make me shut up?' he thundered.

While Mason raged at the audience, five other men, dressed only in red briefs, incanted phrases of despair and enacted the humiliating rituals of the black man's existence in America: slavery; unwarranted police investigations; the white woman's/white America's fantasies about the black man's potency. 'What is the size of Clarence Thomas's penis?' The image of the nearly naked men underscored their historical experience as powerless objects of both desire and barter - but that was an intellectual connection, made with the realisation that their performance offered no real way for me to get inside their anger.

The white media has labelled our work 'angry'. If anger is what it takes to expose the hypocrisy in the art world, in which art institutions pass us on like plantation owners ... the prison farm system for black artists will be developed in the near future like the Nazis spared some Jewish artists whilst in the death camps. The US still controls the world's psyche through its billion dollar industry called Show Business - ask France. And what am I in the mix?

A black art slave on the auction block is no longer loved even in France. Called 'angry' in New York, London, San Francisco, Atlanta, Minneapolis and Los Angeles, I have made powerful enemies because I call a racist a racist. The way in which I have to live as an artist is racist. It just is. My work struggles to end this oppression for myself and others. Who is out there trying to help, I sometimes ask?

The latest attack against my work is 'the cult of personality'. I am personality, that's all. But it is the media who first singled me out of the collective process, and now these white liberal progressive art administrators, friends, on my side, buy in on that ... When I attend art conferences, they warn me against claiming too much credit for the work that I have participated in. They warn what I say is important and people will be influenced by what I say so could I be careful. It feels like a threat. They pull me aside and in secret they tell me I am a wonderful person and artist and I need to be more responsible and more human than even them. So when white audience members feel threatened by the construction of the images and the words in the work ... I know the connection. I learned how it is to be taken personally.

You have read *Revisionist Examination*. The symbols in it are not people ... but how they speak to each other and how they are dressed and what they listen to and how they move were created through my process as a performance artist. This work is done inside a larger performance called *The Undersiege Stories*. The prisoners will watch this play inside their performance. How do I work inside the political and social arena? The US is a prison for me in a personal and private way. I was born in the States when blacks challenged the legal effects of racism. My work does that ... white critics never get that ... they never go there. The issues of jurisprudence ... the ritual of law-making and how the law effects people ... is deeply embedded in my work. When reviewed by the white media they are outraged, hurt, embarrassed by their own reluctance to admit they do not personally understand the work nor enjoy the work on a personal level.

Cathy Curtis, LA Times, 24 February 1990:
When Keith Antar Mason chose the infamous 'wilding'
incident that occurred last year in New York's Central Park as

the basis for a performance piece, he must have realised that he was up against it.

How could anyone of any race summon up a shred of sympathy for the pack of black youths accused of raping and nearly beating to death a white woman jogger?

And yet *Prometheus on a Black Landscape: The Core,* which opened Thursday at Highways in Santa Monica, is full of whining and ranting about the history of black oppression and the frantic needs of the black libido-carrying-ons that, at the very least, make a mockery of black men who have not found it necessary or amusing to deprive others of their liberty...

I wage war, a holy jihad on myself and my beliefs. I write and create images from that personal space. A long time ago, when I was a 'spooky teenage poet', in a philosophy class, I wrote a paper about the world that I was living in. My white teacher wrote back, 'Things aren't that bad anymore.'

He was a white man with a job. I was a black student in a predominantly white school being educated. The white man, the white media, the white art administrator out of control: clear enemies? Some defend cultural democracy, equity, and issues of diversity. They are suspected by both sides. I give them an assignment and they can become the abolitionist of this time period: sign the cheques, install me in your position and go on a quest. A quest to teach other whites about the effects of racism.

If you are not willing to do this, at this critical moment in history, then racism is alive and well in your home, this world. We are fighting a war and winning. Do not tell me otherwise. I am still able to create the image. I am still free and able to nurture other young black artists. I am still free to write. I do this because, I know, we are not supposed even to be alive. My life is a performance. Are you writing out a cheque, searching how to deepen your beliefs in cultural democracy and stepping aside, or are you afraid? Afraid that I even perceive the world this way. Yeah. I am here to stay.

FISHING FOR A NEW RELIGION
(For Lynford French)

Michael McMillan

> Blessed are those who struggle
> Oppression is worse than the grave
> It is better to die for a good cause
> Than to live the life of a slave.[1]

There is a time and place for everything. The emergent debate around black live art reflects the convergence of particular historical conjunctures within the context and discourse of black arts practices in Britain. The black arts cultural renaissance of the 1980s has seen the emergence of a kaleidoscopic range of inter-disciplinary, mixed-media, and fusion-based practices. These, along with debates around identity and representation, and reactions against the European tradition of dividing the arts into different artforms, have shifted the ground in the discourse on art practice and production.

The displacement of the term performance art has coincided with a more general interrogation of representation. 'Cultural diversity' has displaced 'multiculturalism' as the new buzz-word in cultural policy. Black arts practice, traditionally interdisciplinary and politically oppositional, must oppose the dominant regime, which, in its desire to maintain control of the means of cultural production, distribution and circulation, moves the goal-posts by altering definitions whenever it is threatened. A refusal to embrace critical practices has the net result of further perpetuating our marginalisation and leaves a vacuum in our understanding of ourselves, our actions and their impact. It is part of a larger process of identifying the diversity of selves, practices, processes, aesthetics, styles, forms and contents within work.

To talk of black live art practice is to talk of the black arts movement. Like similar movements in cultural history, it has emerged to broaden our understanding of the world, to sensitise us emotionally and intellectually, to challenge the status quo and bring blackness to our consciousness. Like all movements, it will cease once it has achieved its goal.

> If one begins with the threat of concrete nihilism, then one must talk about some kind of politics of conversion... Nihilism is not overcome by arguments or analyses; it is tamed by love and care. Any disease of the soul must be conquered by a turning of one's soul. This turning is done by one's affirmation of one's worth - an affirmation fuelled by the concern of others. This is why a love ethic must be at the center of a politics of conversion.[2]

As cultural workers we are engaged in this politics of conversion and the struggle to develop and practice pedagogies of resistance where the personal becomes political and the political becomes personal.

In African arts and culture, divisions do not exist. Instead, drama, dance, movement, music, the spoken word, poetry, song and visual arts are all fused holistically.

> You know in African tradition the magic happens in the journey *to* the drum. Its not the music that comes from the drum, the drum actually takes you into it.[3]

This phenomenon is not new. It simply reflects the polyphonic nature of black culture as an expression of the fusion of mind, body and spirit. Carnival arts, through the work of artists such as Keith Khan, have been one of the means by which the art world's definitions of form have been undermined. As much as carnival is live art - fusing different disciplines of design, mask, music, dance, song, oral poetry, theatre, performance - it is also a ritual of cultural and political celebration, affirmation and resistance for black communities in Britain, even though it may be appropriated, packaged, commercially exploited and sanitised. The dominant regime's representation of carnival, coded by the image of the exotic rum-drinking-happy-go-lucky-savage, is sustained by a colonial fantasy of fear and desire of the other; fear of carnival's magic and power as a catalyst of collective transformation.

Just as colonialism motivated slaves to re-invent carnival as a ritual of resistance, the Notting Hill Carnival emerged from community activism. In 1965, black settlers took to the streets of London to affirm a nascent post-colonial identity in a neo-colonial society. This shift had previously been signified by race riots in the same area in 1958, in which Kelso Cochrane was murdered. Indeed, the shifts in aesthetics and the struggle for black arts can only be contextualised by looking to the historical conjunctures and cultural politics of black communities.

The ideological and political positions of the Black Power movement provided a motor for black activists and cultural practitioners. In the 1970s and early 1980s, black arts practice emerged as part of a wider response to debates and campaigns against ongoing racist immigration laws, police and state brutality and marginalisation in the housing, education and labour market. These struggles culminated in a number of revolts, from uprisings at the Notting Hill Carnival in 1976 and in the inner cities in 1981 and 1985, to a strike at Grunwick in 1977. The intrinsic relationship between black activism, cultural practices and black communities influenced the idea of 'community' as a construct of community politics which found its expression through the community arts movement.

In Britain's urban centres, subcultural expression in the form of language, dress, style, dance and music has been dominated by black popular culture. This process of cultural exchange is never acknowledged. black DJs *Shut and Dance* re-appropriated the acid/techno/warehouse sound (which had originally been ripped off by the same white soul boys who had appropriated the black-led pirate radio movement of the early 80s), fused techno with dancehall, dub and ragga, and called it Jungle or Jung-list. According to legend, the term Jung-list originated in 'jungle bunny' and 'jungle bunny music'; words used by racist white bouncers on the club scene to describe black DJs, the music they played and the crowd who followed them. Consequently, a pejorative term became re-appropriated, just like 'nigger'.

> The colonised cultures are sliding into the space of the coloniser, and in doing so, they are redefining its borders and its culture ... We need to find a new terminology, a new iconography and a new set of categories and definitions. "We need to re-baptise the world in our own terms. The language of postmodernism is ethnocentric and insufficient. And so is the existing language of cultural institutions and funding agencies. Terms like... 'ethnic', 'minority', 'marginal', 'alternative' and 'Third World' among others are inaccurate and loaded with ideological implications."[4]

Going back to my roots

To talk of black live art practice is to talk of the black arts movement. Like similar movements in cultural history, it has emerged to broaden our understanding of the world, to sensitise us emotionally and intellectually, to challenge the status quo and bring blackness to our consciousness. Like all movements, it will cease once it has achieved its goal.

In Britain, the tradition of black people in theatre has not been of writers or directors, but on stage as part of spectacles that serve colonial fantasies: as menials, slaves and servants. Ira Aldridge, who came to Europe to escape racism in the United States in the 19th century, transcended this tradition in his critically acclaimed portrayal of Othello in 1833, and Oroonoko in *The Revolt of Surinam*, adapted from Thomas Southerne's play (based on a novel by Aphra Behn). Because of racism, he fled England and found recognition and prominence whilst touring throughout Western and Eastern Europe. Ira Aldridge's contribution to the development of the Method School of Acting has not been fully credited.

Michael McMillan

The arrival of Paul Robeson in the 1920s saw racism in British theatre challenged. In both his practice as an actor and his personal activism, Robeson's life prophesied the cultural and political dynamics of a British black arts movement.

> In my music, my plays, my films, I want to carry always this
> central idea: to be African. Multitudes of men have
> died for less worthy ideas; it is even more eminently worth
> living for.[5]

Playing Toussaint L'Ouverture in C L R James' 1936 play, *The Black Jacobins*, he portrayed the experience of colonialism of post-war black settlers from the Caribbean and Africa. This portrayal symbolised the germ of a black theatre in Britain. Post war black theatre accelerated the shift from work which blended 'Western bourgeois aesthetic criteria and a sentimental racial awareness'[6] to the advocation of black 'consciousness', which was reflected in the synthesis of dramaturgical and ideological presuppositions. In the 'mother country', black settlers were here, and their children were here to stay, in search of their own post-colonial identities.

Both the black theatre and community theatre became appropriated into a hierarchically exclusive community arts movement. In the post-*Look Back in Anger* assault on the citadels of British theatre, disaffected middle class and university educated working class practitioners, in their quest for cultural and political redemption, re-constructed their roots through their romantic fight on the front-line of the community activist/agitprop movement. The focus was on working class campaigns, union struggles, women's and other pressure groups, community activism and the democratisation and demystification of arts practice. 'Community' became the site of the socialist revolution which could be hastened if the working class and other disenfranchised communities saw their lives expressed through community arts. The bourgeois notion of a universal community did not include the black community, who could not fit into this neat utopian ideal unless they assimilated its values. The idea of community as a tangible entity, waiting to be led, was a myth, and had to be critiqued.

The community politics which re-emerged - affecting the Greater London Council's increased funding of the arts, and ultimately the development of a community arts sector - was not the community arts movement of old, led by white middle class self-elected representatives of the 'revolutionary masses', but a witness to wider shifts already taking place in the 1980s. As Kobena Mercer, amongst others, has argued, the political events and uprisings of 1981 and 1985 were encoded with militant demands for black representation within public institutions. These institutions subsequently fell over themselves with 'benevolent' gestures that included redistributing funds to black projects. This consolidation of power in the hands of an exclusive community forms part of the colonisation of terms and policies of the 'ethnic arts category'; a backdrop to the nascent development of the black arts sector. Community and cultural politics were revised in the late GLC's campaign for a popular culture. A renaissance of black creativity was thus generated - from literature, music and theatre to photography, film and video.[7]

> ... when you write a play about Black people, white people can assume that this is a finite model of the Black community and that is what the Black community is about. There is a whole range of material available about the white community from *Confessions of a Window Cleaner* to *Apocalypse Now* and it is clear that white society is complex and full of contradictions... White people can afford the luxury of looking at themselves in three dimensions and Black people in two dimensions[8]

The engagement of black theatre practitioners with English theatre, whether in the fringe or mainstream, has to be seen in a wider political framework as an attempt to reposition the guaranteed centres of realism and the classic realist text, in a struggle to contest negative stereotypes with positive representations. Quasi-naturalist/realist aesthetics in black theatre/performance was an overt protest against their marginalisation, and an emphatic insistence on the real to 'correct' the reproduction of colonial fantasies in mis(sed) representations of the black subject and their communities. black theatre, like other black arts practices and discourses, was inscribed with the historical burden of representation. Practitioners were expected to speak for the 'essential real' black

Michael McMillan

community. In this climate of politicised discourse, theatre and performance became limited to ideological issues in a struggle to imagine forms in terms of revolutionary content. Classical theatre circles typically claimed that this type of black community theatre was merely part of the naturalistic/documentary genre, and therefore about people/community issues rather than art or aesthetics.

The struggles of black theatre companies such as Temba, Black Theatre Co-op, Tara Arts, Umoja, Talawa, Double Edge, Roots Theatre, Carib, L'Ouverture and Black Mime Theatre among others, are the struggles of black cultural practitioners to assert the heterogeneous nature of their work. Could solidarity through common struggles be threatened by the diversity of interests generated by identity issues and individual subject positions?

The renaissance of a black arts movement in the 1980s enabled a second generation of black voices that had grown up in Britain to explore questions of identity and representation. Could being black and British be reconciled? Theatre which embraced naturalism and realism was unable to provide the tools necessary to investigate the black experience. As Stuart Hall points out, the politics of representation, identity and subjectivity mark an 'end of innocence' for the essential 'good' black subject (the reversal of which had been the essential 'bad' white subject).

This shift, coupled with a body of writing emerging from cultural studies courses influenced by Gramsci, feminism and black American writers such as Alice Walker and Toni Morrison, signified a privileging of self as the black subject in the process of cultural production. The Theatre of black Women and Munirah were two examples of a ground swell of black women's theatre organisations who told their stories in terms of their gender and sexuality. A counter-discourse of black performance had been constructed that resisted the dominant versions of theatrical reality.

The ritual
The fusion of art forms, use of ritual and what Kwesi Owusu called 'orature', were evident in the work of The Last Poets, Imiri Baraka's *Spirit House Movers*, Ntozake Shange's *For Coloured Girls Who Have Considered Suicide When The Rainbow Was Enuf*,

Double Edge
Theatre Company
Ragamuffin
Photo: Nigel Madhoo,
courtesy of Double Edge
Theatre Company

Michael McMillan

and in plays from the Caribbean, black America and Africa at Keskidee (London's first black arts centre). Much of this work did not reflect a black British experience, until Edgar White's *The Nine Night* juxtaposed the opposing forces in an African-Caribbean family: 'dominoes and chic disco music, curry goat and fish and chips'. In *The Nine Night*,

> we witnessed a refreshing development in the form of the play: there was a fusion of music, dance and drama, especially in the opening 'ritual', which reminded us of the possibilities of exploring and establishing a Black aesthetic in the theatre.[9]

Double Edge's play *Ragamuffin* also displayed this fresh approach to content and form. Ragamuffin was an archetypal young Black urban warrior on trial in a court of African justice, with the defence and prosecution making lyrical social and political commentary over records, in the style of competing MCs. Throughout the proceedings, incidents such as the Haitian Revolution of 1802 and the police killing of Cynthia Jarrett and the ensuing Broadwater Farm riots were presented as evidence. In the tradition of a Sound System's competing posses, the audience became the followers for or against Ragamuffin. The theatre spaces were transformed into the social space of a dancehall, the performing MC calling and the audience responding. Essentially, *Ragamuffin* broke the 'fourth wall' of the proscenium, dividing the audience and the stage and performers. The audience were transformed into a congregation.

This ritualised process is in the tradition of Caribbean popular theatre, a genre imported over the past decade in the form of plays such as *Bups*, *Mama Man* and *Undercover Lover*. All have been loosely called Bups dramas, and dismissed as comic, sexist, and crude, accused of pandering to their audience. But these shows brought black working class audiences to the theatre, where previous black theatre had not. More importantly, audiences here were not alienated by the form or patronised by didactic messages, but felt able to comment, to cuss, to participate, to own, to belong, to reclaim.

> Black theatre is moving to the point where we've taken the ritual, passion, drama and intensity of the church and put it

into secular music so it can be a functional kind of thing; so you can use your catharsis, your collective energy and collective prayer in your everyday life.[10]

Free from the burden of the written narrative and embracing improvisational action and vocality, the relationship between seer and seen, the audience and the performer, the spectator and the artist that is so essential to traditional drama becomes dissolved into the immediacy of ritual. As Molette points out, it becomes 'a total spiritual involvement ... an affirmation of a sense of community.'[11] Ritual, as an improvisational process focusing on word-sounds, chants, musical vibrations and the power of movement, can be seen in the structured spontaneity of jazz.

JAZZOETRY
Rhythms and sounds
In leaps and bounds
Scales and notes and endless quotes
Hey! Black soul being told

Hypnotising while improvising is mentally
Appetising off on a tangent
Ain't got a cent
Searching, soaring, exploring,
    Seek and you shall find
        More time, more time
            More time, more time
                More time, more time[12]

Performance poets have also gone through their own transformations. SuAndi's multi-media performance piece *This Is All I Have To Say* creates an intimate and relaxed environment for the audience using a conversational style of poetry and poignant chat. This is all done as the audience try to digest BNP and Klu Klux Klan propaganda left on their seats, images of black people's resistance to racism are projected and sound bites of BNP and KKK songs are heard. SuAndi's work is in the oral tradition of the African

Visual Stress
Urban Vimbuza **(1988)**
Photo: Kif Higgins

Michael McMillan
and Keith Piper
Portrait of a Shopping
Centre as a
Cathedral **(1991)**
Photo: Ingrid Pollard

griot, who would tell stories and make social commentaries fusing song, drama, dance, music, poetry and disarming humour just as rap artists, ragga MCs and calypsoians do today.

Paul Carter Harrison's critique of 1960s agit-prop/sermonising drama proposed a theatre of spiritual release, which assumes that the spectator is fully aware of the injury to which they are daily subjected. In moving away from material objectivity, black theatre should be judged not on a notion of realism, but by its ability 'to invoke the force of our ancestral spirits' He cites Bantu cosmology in the convergence of time and space using a physical and metaphysical language. It destroys a sense of theatre as spectacle and the inclusion of the 'whole congregation' in ritual activity. 'The event becomes the context reality, a force-field of phenomena which is ritualised'. The performance rises out of the audience and develops through open and closed audience permission, finally flowing into 'communal will' What the spectator at first witnesses they will ultimately become; inclusion and participation are not mere metaphors, but concrete physical acts.

> The audience must control the space, and feel that it is their space. Within this conceptualisation of the process of ritual, the stage/barrier is transcended and transformed creating an nbroken circle of participants/activators as performers. And, as found in many cultures, the circle as ritual concept is a metaphor of collective transformation and the never ending cycle of life.[13]

As a witness to Visual Stress' *Urban Vimbuza*, I saw further possibilities of ritual as a subversive process. Liverpool's Saint George's Plateau, a civic monument to colonial adventure, became the site of a mystical shamanistic urban ritual to heal the city, raising questions of territory, ownership, control and identity in the process. Visual Stress took advantage of the euphoria that surrpounded a week-end set aside to honour John Lennon to re-invent the city, subverting it with cultural warfare.

The personal is political

My own roots as a writer and theatre practitioner lie in black community theatre practice. Much of my early work was an attempt to question, challenge and provoke. The damage inflicted during the 1980s by fascistic Thatcherite market forces, which caused cuts in funding across the theatre sector, had its greatest effect on the flourishing black theatre movement. Theatre companies took less risks, and made work that guaranteed 'bums on seats' rather than take the risk of providing a platform for black British writers with new ideas (- white-run institutions tend to import supposedly 'safe' work from the African Diaspora). Disillusioned with the strait-jacket of black theatre's conventionality, and desiring to take risks with politicised performance, I was influenced by critical debates in cultural studies, film theory and black visual arts and stumbled upon performance art. Collaborating with mixed-media artist Keith Piper on *Portrait of a Shopping Centre as a Cathedral* - a site specific performance installation - was a liberating experience. Performed in Dalston Cross shopping centre, Hackney in October 1990, it parodied the appropriation of black popular culture in the commodification of lifestyle: high top sports boots, subversive dress styles and street-wise attitudes.

Portrait of a Shopping Centre explored the shopping centre/mall as a kind of cathedral or modern holy relic. Deconstructing today's commodity and consumption-oriented society, it examined how the role once occupied by the cathedral as the literal and physical embodiment of the power and pre-eminence of the church, has been co-opted by the shopping centre, which seduces and enslaves us with consumer commodities elevated to the status of contemporary icons. The United Colours of Benetton advertising campaign echoed an image of the United Nations reminiscent of Coca-Cola's famous hill-top advertisement which showed young people in their national costumes, representing some 30 countries ('I'd like to buy the world a home, and furnish it with love, grow apple trees and honey bees and snow-white turtle doves... I'd like to buy the world a coke ...'[14]).

Parodying the hard-sell routine of the marketplace, two performers attempted to sell the installation to shoppers and passers-by. The action simultaneously highlighted the ironies of a commercial space absent of black businesses, next to one of only two African-

Caribbean markets in London. Like a congregation, spectators participated in the collective ritual of reading our community prayer through call and response, completing the meaning of the piece itself:

> Our shopping centre which art in Dalston,
> Hallowed by thy enterprise.
> our money come,
> our money go
> in Hackney as it is in the city.
> Give us our daily bread - pound, shilling and pence,
> lead us not into more debt,
> but forgive those that send reminders,
> for thine is the bank statement,
> interest free credit and the discount,
> until it runs out.
> But
> never, never
> our people
> Amen.[15]

The job of the artist, as Guillermo Gómez-Peña has said, is to force open the matrix of reality to admit unsuspected possibilities.[16] As a writer in theatre, performance and mixed-media, language is the tool (both tweezer and crowbar) that I use to open these worlds. Language - its meaning, its subversion, its transformation - whether verbal, textual, physical, spiritual, meta-physical - is the means by which I communicate change.

> language is a point of reference
> it's what I use when I write
> like my forebears' wisdom
> like my skin the night
>
> that covers my overspending
> and help me not miss

> the how/why/the wherefore
> of speaking like this[17]

Black masculinity

Created whilst I was working with Double Edge, *Invisible* is a solo multi-media piece inspired by Ralph Ellison's novel *The Invisible Man* and Frantz Fanon's *Black Skin, White Masks*. *Invisible* explored ancient African ritual arts from a contemporary avant garde perspective.

In questioning the invisibility of the black subject, the internalisation of the self-as-other, as exotic, as primitive, as savage, as colonised, *Invisible* posited a post-colonial paradigm:

> I celebrate my irresponsibility,
> for I am able to see you
> while you cannot see me,
> and in doing so,
> I move between the cracks in time,
> the gaps in space,
> read me between the lines,
> I'm there.
>
> Sleepwalkers!
> You must pay the price
>
> What did I do to be so blue?
> Bear with me.
>
> Who knows, maybe on the lower frequencies,
> I speak for me and for you.
> I know myself, do you?[18]

In the form of a fragmented narrative, *Invisible* explored the black man's need to interrogate his comfortable realities. Using video and sound projection, it deliberately challenged perceptions.

Pomo Afro Homos
Dark Fruit (1991)
Photo: Jill Posener

Michael McMillan

When three black gay men formed performance group Pomo Afro Homos (Post-Modern African-American Homosexuals), black theatre companies in the United States chose to deny their existence and the group were subsequently banned from the National Black Theatre Festival in Winston-Salem, North Carolina (1991). Black theatre must embrace diversity and difference amongst its practices, learn to incorporate cultural, political and personal agendas. Pomo Afro Homos, through short sketches using drama, song, dance and some serious snapping, take a challenging look at the struggles black gay men face in defining their community and sexuality. The company were invited to perform *Dark Fruit* in Newcastle in 1991 as part of a week-long series of events that culminated in a residency I was doing on HIV/Aids in the North East of England with The Artist's Agency. Whilst trying to secure London dates at a black-based venue, I came up against indifference and feeble excuses, suggestive of a silent homophobia.

Pomo Afro Homos have something to say, not simply to gay communities but to black men in general. Many black cultural commentators - self-appointed community gurus - talk of the genocide going on in the black community, about black men killing black men, black men being criminalised, black men internalising stereotypes, black men taking out the same form of abuse they experience on the women of the community. Pomo Afro Homos talk frankly about sex, sexuality, love, relationships and fathering as a healing process. It is work which both critiques and reclaims our own masculinity.

I recently collaborated in a workshop for black men with The Hittite Empire, an LA-based black male ensemble whose mixed-media performances break the silence of our private and public truths. For the participants, the journey was creative, while at the same time emotionally empowering and healing.

> We must have the courage to turn our gaze inward and begin to raise the touchy issues that most of us avoided in the past decade: Men of colour are active participants in the history of sexism and (European) women share the blame in the history of racism. We must accept this with valour and dignity.[19]

As Frantz Fanon, in *Black Skin, White Masks,* argues, myths about the violent, aggressive and 'animalistic' nature of black sexuality were fabricated and fictioned by the white master to allay his fears and anxieties, and provide a means to justify the brutalisation of the colonised.[20] These fictions of the sexually active savage have entered the social construction of black masculinity today. Power, control and authority as prevailing definitions of masculinity were historically denied to the black man, consequently there emerges the contradictory formation of a subordinated masculinity. A further turn of the screw of oppression comes with the black male subjectively internalising and incorporating aspects of the dominant definition of masculinity, to contest the conditions of dependency and powerlessness. Many of the assumptions about black sexuality emanate from a view of the black family as deviant, dysfunctional, disorganised and pathological: a family that fails to socialise their offspring into the correct societal norms. The reproduction of the ideology of Africans as so called 'high risk groups' coincides with the representation of African-Caribbean men in the press in terms of HIV transmission.

Unlike black women, no heterosexual black men got involved in the HIV/Aids residency in the North East. The dominant HIV/Aids discourse is racist, and in the future, black cultural practitioners, as they become infected or affected through friends, family and lovers or get fed up with the fear, prejudice and demonology surrounding this epidemic, will get involved. But let us be under no illusions, it is not about soft, simple, safe cultural responses, but hard-core cultural interventions. I began to see my role in the process of the residency not simply as an artist, but a cultural activist.

The black family is synonymous with community, but until the families, friends and lovers affected by HIV/Aids begin to break the deafening silence of denial and blame, then lamentations will continue to resonate for those *individuals* affected: 'Deliver me from mine enemies, oh my God... the mighty are gathered against me: not for my transgressions, not for my sin.[21]

Let us heal with praise-songs to ancestors, to those funky brothers and sisters who chose to be different when others conformed, who chose to question when others remained silent, who challenged, subverted and were made lepers by their own communities. Don't

(For Lynford French)

believe the hype. We don't all look the same and cook the same.

As Brecht argued, art is not truly revolutionary unless it is revolutionary in form. If Sojourner Truth's struggles gave rise to the feminist movement, then we can achieve likewise. Black artists in performance and mixed-media are already reconstructing, re-appropriating, re-inventing the avant garde as they cross the border between art and cultural politics.

> The avant garde is no longer in the front but in the margins. To be avant garde... is to contribute to the decentralisation of art. To be avant garde means to be able to cross the border back and front between art and politically significant territory, be it inter-racial, immigration, ecology, homelessness, Aids or violence towards disenfranchised communities and Third World countries. To be avant garde means to perform and exhibit in both artistic and non-artistic contexts: to operate in the world, not just the art world.[22]

Word Up!

1   The Last Poets, *Vibes from the Scribes* (Pluto, London, 1985)

2   Cornel West, *Nihilism in Black America*, quoted in bell hooks' 'Dialectically Down with the Critical Program' in *Black Popular Culture* (Bay Press, Seattle, 1992)

3   Linda Burham, 'Yo! Its the End of the World: On LA Artist Keith Antar Mason' in High Performance, Summer 1989, Los Angeles

4   Guillermo Gómez-Peña, 'The Multi-Cultural Paradigm, An Open Letter to the National Arts Community' in High Performance, Fall 1989, Los Angeles

5   Kwesi Owusu, *The Struggle for Black Arts in Britain* (Commedia, London, 1986)

6   Kimberly W Benston, 'The Aesthetic of Modern Black Drama' in *The Theatre of Black Americans*, ed. Errol Hill (Applause, New York 1987)

7   Kobena Mercer and Isaac Julien, 'Race, Sexual Politics and Black Masculinity' in *Male Order: Unwrapping Masculinity*, ed. Rowena Chapman and Jonathan Rutherford (Lawrence & Wishart, London, 1988)

8   Sindamani Bridglal, 'Profile of Caryl Phillips' in Artrage Vol. 1, November 1982, London

9   Owusu, *op. cit.*

10 Geneva Smitherman, 'We Are The Music: Ron Milner, People's Playwright' in Benston, *op.cit.*

11 P Molette, as quoted in Benston, *op. cit.*

12 The Last Poets, *op.cit.*

13 Paul Carter Harrison, as quoted in Benston, *op. cit.*

14 Text from Michael McMillan and Keith Piper, *Portrait of a Shopping Centre as a Cathedral*, a multi-media performance event at Dalston Cross shopping centre, commissioned by Art & Society in 1991

15 Michael McMillan and Keith Piper, *op. cit.*

16 Guillermo Gómez-Peña, 'Hybrid America' in Hybrid No. 5 (National Review of Live Art catalogue), October 1993, London

17 Lynford French, 'Over Understanding' in *Her/Story So Far*, ed Black Ink (London 1983)

18 *Invisible*, Double Edge Theatre Company (1993)

19 Gómez-Peña, Hybrid, *op.cit.*

20 Frantz Fanon, *Black Skin, White Masks* (Pluto Press, London 1986) and Robert Staples, *Black Masculinity: The Black Male's Role in American Society* (Black Scholar Press, Oakland 1982)

21 Michael McMillan, 'Art as a verb' in *Living Proof: Views of the World Living with HIV and Aids* (Artist's Agency, Newcastle 1992)

22 Gómez-Peña, High Performance, *op. cit.*

210

Performance   bell hooks
practice as a site
of opposition

PERFORMANCE PRACTICE AS A SITE OF OPPOSITION
bell hooks

Walking around the streets of New York City we see many homeless black people engaged in ritualistic performative acts. Some of them have routines that they repeat over and over to passers-by: narratives about death and destruction, about Babylon, the evil white people have done black folks, and how they must suffer for it. These homeless individuals are rarely begging. They are possessed spirits. In another culture - not a white supremacist, capitalist, patriarchal nation - their words might be listened to, their wisdom heeded. Their presence in every city in the United States speaks to the problematic nature of African-American performance, live art and related practices in the West today. They embody the amalgamation of ancient traditions, where one performed, especially during rites of possession, for ritual purposes or to use the notion of manipulative performance for survival. This grew out of plantation culture and the experience of slavery. These two contradictory modes of performance merge and become madness. This madness articulates aspects of African-American post-modern identity - the absence of community, alienation from everyday reality, a fragmented individuality, and the loss of organised resistance - struggles that reach masses of black people across class.

Thinking about the history of African-American engagement with performance-as-art, it is useful to distinguish between performance that is used to manipulate in the interests of survival (the notion of wearing a mask), and performance as ritual play (as art). Collapsing the two categories tends to imply that the performative arts in black expressive culture emerge as a response to circumstances of oppression and exploitation. It is useful to consider these two modes of performance as both similar and different. One may engage in strategic performances in the interests of survival employing the same

Throughout African-American history, performance has been crucial in the struggle for liberation, precisely because it has not required the material resources demanded by other artforms. The voice as instrument could be used by everyone, in any location.

skills one uses to perform in the interest of ritual play, yet the performative standpoint alters both the nature and impact of the performance. In one context performance can easily become an act of complicity, in the other, it can serve as critical intervention, as a rite of resistance.

As young black children raised in the post slavery southern culture of apartheid, we were taught to appreciate and participate in 'live arts'. Organised stage shows were one of the primary places where we were encouraged to display talent. Dramatic readings of poetry, monologues, or plays were all central in these shows. Whether we performed in church or school, these displays of talent were seen as both expressions of artistic creativity and as political challenges to racist assumptions about the creative abilities of black folks. We performed for ourselves as subjects, not as objects seeking approval from the dominant culture. In our all-black schools and churches, performance was a place of celebration, a ritual play wherein one announced liberatory subjectivity.

Throughout African-American history, performance has been crucial in the struggle for liberation, precisely because it has not required the material resources demanded by other artforms. The voice as instrument could be used by everyone, in any location. In my household we staged performances in our living room, reciting poetry and acting in written or improvised drama.

The spoken word, transformed into a performed act, remains a democratic cultural terrain. When and where institutional structures were not available for individual black folks, we used, and still use, street corners, barbershops, beauty parlours, basketball courts and a host of other locations in order to be in on the live act.

All performance practice has, for African-Americans, been central to the process of decolonisation in white supremacist capitalist patriarchy. From times of slavery to the present day, the act of claiming voice, of asserting both one's right to speak as well as saying what one wants to say, has been a challenge to those forms of domestic colonisation that seek to over-determine the speech of those who are exploited and/or oppressed. Performance was important because it created a cultural context where one could transgress the boundaries of accepted speech, both in relationship to the dominant white culture, and to the decorum of African-American cultural mores. Although not talked about as much as it should be, the movement for racial uplift that had its roots in nineteenth century black bourgeois culture, placed such a premium on decorum and correct behaviour that it restricted speech and action. Performance practice was one of the places where the boundaries created by the emphasis on proving that the black race was not uncivilised could be disrupted. Radical ideas could be expressed in this arena. Indeed, the roots of black performative arts emerge from an early nineteenth century emphasis on oration and the recitation of poetry. In a number of narratives relating slave experience, African-Americans cite learning to read and recite as crucial to their development of a liberatory consciousness.

The poetry of the Harlem Renaissance, like much of the fiction of that period, sought to reclaim vernacular speech as the voice of resistance. It did that through an insistence on the production of work that could be performed. The poetry of Langston Hughes epitomises this emphasis on recitation. In poems like *The Dream Deferred*, where the writer shifts back and forth between standard English, dialect and patois, one cannot hear the distinct voices in his work unless these works are read aloud - performed.

When tracing their artistic development, African-American women writers such as Maya Angelou often call attention to those formative years in school, where they learned to recite. Victimised by both racism and sexism, pushed into silence, Angelou recovered her voice - and with it her sanity, her capacity to face reality - by learning to perform. In the recent biography of James Earle Jones, the actor's development is charted as the movement from being someone who was afraid to speak (in part because he stuttered) to that moment when he is compelled by a teacher to learn a poem that he must perform in front of the class. No black fiction writer has mapped the place of black expressive culture in everyday life as a site of resistance as succinctly as the African-Caribbean-American writer Paule Marshall. In *Praisesong For The Widow* she weaves a tapestry of the black expressive culture that permeates the life of an upwardly-mobile, black, working class family. Listening to music, reciting poems in everyday life, they keep in touch with the distinct creative power of their experience, and the cultural legacy of Diaspora black life, from Africa, the Caribbean, and the United States.[1]

Reading this novel in class, I have found that students express disbelief that recitation of poetry would be so central to a working class black family. Yet I grew up in a working class family, where the particular skills of black art expressed in writing poetry were honoured through the act of performance. We were encouraged to learn the works of black poets, to recite them to one another. In daily life, this was both a means of sharing our cultural legacy and of resisting indoctrination from Eurocentric biases within educational systems that devalued black expressive culture.

Clearly the performing arts have been crucial to the process by which we, as African-Americans, decolonise our minds and imaginations. It is useful to think in terms of ethnographic performance when charting a cultural history of African-American participation in the performing arts. Critic Jill MacDougall, in an article discussing the plays of Lebanese woman writer Abla Farhoud, entitled *Growing... Growing... Growing... Growing.. Growing... Growing... Growing... Growing... Analysis of a Work-in-Progress*, clarifies her understanding of this phrase:

> As a displaced person moving between cultures, I am viewing identity as a work-in-progress, a disappearing act, a performance. As a performer, director, linguist, and translator, I am considering ethnography as a negotiation of meanings, as open and infinite semiotic chain, an ongoing activity rather than a stable definition. In other words, I am

> emphasising the act of doing, rather than the immobile
> quality contained in the lexeme 'ethnography'.

Drawing on MacDougall's analysis, I would see most African-American performance practice as a critical ethnography because it usually represents individual experience in ways that, as she suggests 'metonymically refer to, but can never grasp, an entire culture'. Hence it is always a partial truth, 'subjective and incomplete' that uses polyphonic strategies to convey specific aspects of black experience.

These strategies of performance are most evident in the work of contemporary black artist Anna Deavere Smith. In the introduction to *Fires In the Mirror*, Cornel West describes her work as a 'great example of how art can constitute a public space that is perceived by people as empowering rather than disempowering.'[2] Of course, it is the particular artistic medium she has chosen that makes this sense of empowerment possible. Performance as ritual re-enactment is quintessentially highlighted in Deveare Smith's work because she draws on current events and on the actual statements of a range of observers present at those events. This strategy of re-enactment has been at the core of African-American performance practice. The sense of immediacy is there not because art intrinsically functions in the manner West describes, rather it is present precisely because performance art and performance artists invoke that sense of immediacy by working critically to intervene in public response to events, in ways that are empowering. For Smith's work to be effective as critical intervention, the re-enactment must occur in the wake of the actual events. Performed at a distance from the events the work describes, it would lose its power to act as a critical intervention. It would become a cultural product, consumed without the kind of critical engagement that might engender a response beyond that of merely good or bad performance. As Peggy Phelan contends in *Unmarked: the politics of performance,*

> Performance's only life is in the present. Performance cannot
> be saved, recorded, documented, or otherwise participate in
> the circulation of representations *of* representations: once it
> does so, it becomes something other than performance. To

the degree that performance attempts to enter the economy of reproduction it betrays and lessens the promise of its own ontology. Performance's being, like the ontology of subjectivity proposed here, becomes itself through disappearance.[3]

All African-American engagement in the performing arts, whether through the staged performance of poetry and plays, or through rap, risks losing its power to disrupt and engage with the specific locations from which it emerges via a process of commodification that requires reproduction in a marketable package. As mass product, live performance can rarely address the local in a meaningful way, because the primacy of addressing the local is sacrificed to the desire to engage a wider audience of paying consumers.

The power of African-American performance in relation to advocating and advancing the black liberation struggle has been enormous. During the sixties, much political education for critical consciousness was done in popular culture through the live act. Here, I want to speak not just about the radical poets, and/or musicians whose work jolted many of us into consciousness: Ritchie Havens, Don L Lee (known now as Haki Madubuti), Le Roi Jones (known now as Amiri Baraka), Nikki Giovanni etc.; I would also include political leaders like Martin Luther King and Malcolm X whose orations were performance art. Their speeches were powerful and moving, not solely because of the way they put words together on the page or extemporaneously; it was the way that they 'performed' those words that deeply affected the listener.

A few years ago in an interview that first appeared in *Angry Women*, an anthology published by RE/search, I talked about the way in which I saw my lectures as performances, stating that I had learned the primacy of performance when growing up. 'In traditional black culture, if you get up in front of an audience, you should be performing, you should be capable of moving people, something should take place - there should be some total experience. If you got up in front of an audience and were just passively reading something - well, what's the point?' I was emphasising the way in

Martin Luther King (1963)
Photo courtesy of
Hulton Deutsch

**Malcolm X speaks
in Harlem**
Photo courtesy of
Hulton Deutsch

which performance as art was revered in traditional black culture. That sense of reverence is sustained wherever black folks live and create. It was expected of any person who wanted to use words to reach people that they would learn to offer those works in the most compelling performative manner. The point of this performance is to engage an audience in such a way that they not only participate but, potentially, are transformed in some way. In this interview I shared this perspective on performance, that it was about 'total engagement - an engagement that also suggests dialogue and reciprocity between the performer and the audience...'[4] Increasingly the commodification of the performing arts, which seeks to extend work beyond the power of its immediate and often spontaneous setting, promotes passivity and negates this call for reciprocal engagement. When folks came to hear the words of King and Malcolm X they were engaged in concrete liberation struggle. The issue was not creating a marketable commodity, it was to create a liberatory consciousness in a disenfranchised colonised group of people. Both these leaders were concerned with reaching a mass audience, with talking to those most exploited and/or oppressed. Their longing to reach the masses determined the nature of their performance, the works they chose and the way they spoke those words. These orators really showed the method in which performance art could serve a meaningful role in liberation struggle.

If African-American engagement with the performing arts is to sustain its role as a site of pedagogical resistance, where knowledge that educates folks for critical consciousness is shared through performance, then there has to be a recognition of the importance of localised work. Nowadays, individual black folks engaged in performance practice, who are inspired by radical political commitment to social change, face a culture where blackness is increasingly commodified in ways that undermine the power of performance as ritual play which also functions as a site of resistance. In the past the central audience for African-American performance was primarily black people. Reaching diverse audiences widens the scope of influence and contact, making it possible for black performance artists to engage in coalition building - in the formation of new communities. In his introduction to *Fires In The Mirror*, Cornel West reminds us that 'public performance has a unique capacity to bring us together - to take us out of our tribal mentalities - for self critical examination and artistic pleasure.'[5] Of course, as one seeks to interest a wider audience, the nature of material and performance alters. More and more individual black performance artists fashion their work so that it appeals primarily to white consumers. Black performance and related practice has yet to be fully theorised in a manner that would enable discussion of the way in which desire to reach a specific audience shapes the nature of standpoint and perspective. At times the performance work of individuals (like Anna Deavere Smith, Adrian Piper, Coco Fusco to name a few) appears to be specifically designed to disrupt mainstream white sensibilities. While this work is effective and fulfils a need for critical intervention in that arena, it is equally important to maintain a space within various localised arenas of African-American culture, where performance continues to address the specific realities of black experience, as well as the need for a continued black liberation struggle.

Whenever we choose performance as a site to build communities of resistance we must be able to shift paradigms and styles of performance in a manner that centralises the decolonisation of black minds and imaginations, even if we include everyone else in that process. The politicisation of historical memory in performance practice, the recognition of diverse black experience and Diaspora connections between black folks globally, all contribute to sustaining the spirit of radicalism in contemporary black performance. Recently, Cornel West and I spoke to an audience of thousands who had paid to come and hear the two of us dialogue together. The critical intellectual dialogues we engage in publicly are 'performances'. Individuals come to watch the way our interaction with each other creates a narrative as much as they come to hear the political content of what we say. On this particular evening we addressed an audience in New York City that was diverse in every way. Significantly, although the high school auditorium was packed, and temperatures were incredibly hot, the audience was eager to stay for hours to engage with us. Moments like this one indicate how much unmediated direct engagement with an audience, in its diverse forms, remains a place where we can educate for critical consciousness; where communities of resistance can emerge.

African-American performance has always been a space where folks come together and experience the fusion of pleasure and critical pedagogies, a space that aims to subvert and challenge white supremacy as a system of institutionalised domination, along with class elitism, and more lately, sexism. Recent critiques of identity politics, which have traditionally informed African-American performance practice, call us to interrogate the limitation of an emphasis on shared experience. Yet it would be a mistake for black performance artists to surrender the focus on radical subjectivity that has marked performance as a space of transgression. My perspective is akin to that of Jill Dolan who emphasises, in her collection of essays *Presence and Desire: Essays on Gender, Sexuality, Performance*, that she is,

> unwilling and unable to give up identity, however constructed, positional, and unstable, as a place from which to begin my work - not as an ontologically meaningful home and a safe, idealised origin, but as a place of material circumstance that has deeply marked my own embodiments and movements through culture and discourse.[6]

Dolan highlights the two aspects of her identity - being lesbian and Jewish - that she feels must be reclaimed. For African-Americans, performance has been a place where we have reclaimed subjugated knowledge and historical memory. Along with this, it has also been a space of transgression where new identities and radicalised black subjectivities emerge, illuminating our place in history in ways that challenge and interrogate, that highlight the shifting nature of black experience. African-American performance has been a site for the imagination of future possibilities. Importantly, for performance to continue to be subversive, to engage cultural practice in ways that are disruptive and transformative, African-American artists must claim a space for ongoing critical vigilance, where we can dialogue about the impact of the live act and where performance can be interrogated to see what works as meaningful intervention.

African-American performance artists have always played a primary role in the process of collective black political self-recovery, in both the process of decolonisation and the imagining and construction of liberatory identities. It has been a space where communities of resistance are forged to sustain us, a place where we know we are not alone. To retain that radical potential, to realise it, the performing arts in black life cannot surrender to the impetus to engage audiences. The emphasis on reciprocity in African-American performance has marked this as a site that can challenge and transform. As Phelan contends in *Unmarked,*

> Performance implicates the real through the presence of living bodies. In performance art spectatorship there is an element of consumption: there are no left-overs, the gazing spectator must try to take everything in. Without a copy, live performance plunges into visibility - in a maniacally charged present - and disappears into memory, into the realm of invisibility and the unconscious where it eludes regulation and control ... performance art is vulnerable to charges of valuelessness and emptiness. Performance indicates the possibility of revaluing that emptiness; this potential revaluation gives performance art its distinctive oppositional edge.[7]

Performance artists are here to stay, yet it is uncertain whether or not they will continue to function in a radical way. Right now, reclaiming and maintaining African-American performance practice as a site of opposition is the crucial agenda.

1   Paule Marshall, *Praisesong for the Widow* (Dutton, New York 1989)

2   Cornel West in introduction to *Fires in the Mirror* by Anna Deavere Smith

3   Peggy Phelan, *Unmarked: the politics of performance* (Routledge, London 1993)

4   bell hooks, interviewed by Andrea Juno in Angry Women, RE/search #13, San Francisco 1991

5   Cornel West, op. cit.

6   Jill Dolan, *Presence and Desire: essays on gender, sexuality, performance* (University of Michigan Press, Ann Arbor 1993)

7   Peggy Phelan, op. cit.

NOTES ON CONTRIBUTORS

Keith Antar Mason

Keith Antar Mason is a Los Angeles-based writer, performance artist, poet, playwright and cultural activist. He is an interdisciplinary artist who has been performing his own works in a variety of media since 1979. Co-founder and Artistic Director of The Hittite Empire, he aims to create political theatre that serves the black communities in America and the world. The Hittite Empire have performed throughout America and recently staged their work in London. Live works include: *Black Folks and Heroes, Sexual Illegals, The Undersiege Stories, Shango Walks Through Fire* and *Icarus Looking Back*. He is the founder of blackmadrid, a black poetry-jazz-rap-griot recording collective that has created works for New American Radio, BarKubCo Music and New Alliance Records. He is on the steering committee of the National Performance Network (NPN) and active in numerous arts organisations and African-American community concerns nationally and locally.

Nina Edge

Primarily a visual artist based in Liverpool, Nina Edge also participates in carnival and interdisciplinary performance-based events. Recent exhibitions include: *Virtual Duality* (Bluecoat Arts Centre, Liverpool), *Ethnic Cleansing* (Grand Hall, Liverpool) *Batik* (Portsmouth Arts Centre). Recent performance works include: *MILAP* (Bluecoat, Liverpool) and *Kali and Liberty* (Liverpool City of Architecture bid). She was a performance participant in *Zong* by Visual Stress (Maritime Museum, Liverpool), and collaborated on *Prontowipe Bulk Erazer* with artist and curator Mike Stubbs (Hull Time Based Arts and Royal Festival Hall, London).

Coco Fusco

Coco Fusco is a Los Angeles-based interdisciplinary artist and writer. Her essays have appeared in Art in America, The Village Voice, The Los Angeles Times, Third Text, amongst other publications. Fusco has performed, exhibited and lectured throughout the US, Europe, Latin America, Canada, Australia and South Africa. Together with Guillermo Gómez-Peña she has created *Mexarcane International* (1994), *The Year of The White Bear* (1992) and *Norte:Sur* (1990) - arts projects that include multi-media installation, audio art, performances and video. Since 1987, Fusco has curated nine film and video programmes in the US, Europe and Latin America. She co-produced the video documentaries *Havana Postmodern: The New Cuban Art* and *The Couple in the Cage*, and is currently directing a new video, *Pochonovela*, featuring the comedians of Chicano Secret Service. She is a 1994 Mellon Fellow at the California Institute for the Arts. A collection of her essays and scripts, entitled *English Is Broken Here*, will be published in May 1995 by The New Press.

Paul Gilroy

Paul Gilroy is a London-based writer and lecturer. He currently teaches at Goldsmiths' College, University of London and Yale University. He is author of *There Ain't No Black in the Union Jack* (1987), *The Black Atlantic* (1993), *Small Acts* (1994) and co-author of *The Empire Strikes Back* (1982). He is currently working on a new book about fascism.

bell hooks

bell hooks is Distinguished Professor of English at City College in New York, as well as a writer, artist and cultural activist who speaks widely on issues of race, class, and gender. She is author of *Killing Rage, Ending Racism* (1995), *Outlaw Culture* (1994), *Teaching to Transgress: Education as the Practice of Freedom* (1993), *Black Looks: Race, Gender and Cultural Politics* (1992), *Yearning: Race, Gender and Culture* (1990), *Talking Back* (1989), and *Feminist Theory: From Margin To Center* (1984).

Shishir Kurup

Shishir Kurup is a writer, director, performer and musician. Born in Bombay, India, raised in Mombassa, Kenya, he currently lives in Los Angeles and considers himself an Indo-African-American. His solo works *Assimilation* and *Exile: Ruminations on a Reluctant Martyr* have been staged in America and the UK. He is a Suzuki Instructor at UC Irvine's Drama Department. Co-Director with Page Leong of Raven Group and a member of Cornerstone Theater Company, his most recent works for Cornerstone include: *Ghurba*, which he wrote and directed for the Los Angeles Festival and *Everyman in the Mall*, on which he co-directed and composed music. He directed *The Barking Wall* and his self-authored *Skeleton Dance* for Raven Group at the Los Angeles Theatre Center.

Michael McMillan

Michael McMillan is a writer, theatre practitioner and mixed-media artist. He has worked extensively in arts programming, community publishing and arts education. Recent live works include: *Portrait of a shopping centre as a Cathedral*, a site specific performance installation in collaboration with Keith Piper, Dalston Cross shopping centre, and *The Last Blind Date Show* for North East Aids Week. Artistic Director of Double Edge Theatre Company (a black theatre performance company) for two years, he wrote *Invisible*, a multi-media performance piece inspired by Ralph Ellison's *Invisible Man*. A cultural critic, writing extensively on black theatre, performance and live art practice in Britain, his published works include *Cultural Grounding: Live Art and Cultural Diversity*. He is currently Researcher for Manchester Metropolitan University's Live Writing Project.

Catherine Ugwu

Catherine Ugwu is currently Deputy Director of Live Arts at the Institute of Contemporary Arts, London, holding programming, curatorial and commissioning responsibilities. She has been involved in the area of performance and related practice since 1986, both on the ICA's staff and working freelance with a range of arts organisations and companies including The Albany Empire Theatre, Cheek By Jowl Theatre Company, Black Theatre Co-operative, Chisenhale Dance Space, The National Review of Live Art and Islington International Festival. She has been a dance advisor for The London Arts Board for three years and is a member of the advisory board of The Showroom Gallery, London. In 1993 she organised the State of the Art Conference as part of the National Review of Live Art, which addressed issues of cultural diversity and live art practice, and has contributed to national and international conferences.